UNIVERSITY CASEBOOK SERIES®

DISCUSSION PROBLEMS FOR FEDERAL INCOME TAXATION

SEVENTH EDITION

DANIEL L. SIMMONS
Professor of Law Emeritus
University of California at Davis

MARTIN J. MCMAHON, JR.
James J. Freeland Eminent Scholar in Taxation
Professor of Law Emeritus
University of Florida

BRADLEY T. BORDEN
Professor of Law
Brooklyn Law School

DENNIS J. VENTRY, JR.
Professor of Law
University of California at Davis

FOUNDATION
PRESS

University Casebook Series is a trademark registered in the U.S. Patent and Trademark Office.

© 2017 LEG, Inc. d/b/a West Academic
    444 Cedar Street, Suite 700
    St. Paul, MN 55101
    1-877-888-1330

Printed in the United States of America

ISBN: 978-1-60930-265-8

PREFACE

These problems are designed to give students exposure to working with the concepts and statutory provisions studied in Simmons, McMahon, Borden & Ventry, FEDERAL INCOME TAXATION, CASES AND MATERIALS (7th ed.). These problems reflect our experience teaching from the materials in the casebook.

The problem sets are coordinated to the Chapters and Sections in the casebook to which they relate. Some problems will require students to study and apply the Code and regulations, while others will require extrapolation or reasoning by analogy from cases and other materials covered in the reading. Nevertheless, all of the problems pertain specifically to material covered in the casebook and the correct responses can be found from those materials or the relevant portions of the Code and regulations.

We are grateful Professor Alice Abreu, our co-author on the fifth edition, and Professor Gregg Polsky, our co-author on the sixth edition of the casebook, for their enormous contributions to this problem set.

Our work on these problems is never finished. We appreciate all comments and suggestions for improvements. Please send those comments and suggestions to brad.borden@brooklaw.edu.

DANIEL L. SIMMONS
MARTIN J. MCMAHON
BRADLEY T. BORDEN
DENNIS J. VENTRY, JR.

July 1, 2017

TABLE OF CONTENTS

PART I INTRODUCTION TO FEDERAL INCOME TAXATION 1

Chapter 1. Introduction...1
Section 1. An Overview of Policy Issues and the Current Income Tax 1
    A. Selection of a Tax—Goals and Criteria...1
    B. The Structure of the Income Tax and Selected Policy Issues..........................2
Section 2. The Road to the Sixteenth Amendment and the Modern Federal
        Income Tax 2
Section 3. The Federal Income Tax System and the Modern
        Federal Income Tax 2
    A. The Legislative Process..2
    B. The Administrative Process...3
    C. The Judicial Process...3
    E. The Tax Adviser..3

PART II GROSS INCOME...5

Chapter 2. General Principles of Gross Income 5
Section 1. Income 5
    A. Increase in Net Worth...5
    B. Indirect Receipts..6
Section 2. The Realization Requirement 6
Section 3. Imputed Income..7

Chapter 3. Compensation for Services 9
Section 1. Noncash Economic Gains...9
Section 2. Employee Fringe Benefits...10
    A. Statutory Exclusions Based on Tax Policy and Administrative
       Convenience...10
    B. Employee Benefits Excluded from Gross Income to Further
       Social Policy Goals...11

Chapter 4. Gifts, Inheritances and Similar Items 12
Section 1. Gifts and Inheritances 12
Section 2. Life Insurance Death Benefits...13
Section 3. Prizes 14
Section 4. Scholarships...14
Section 5. Governmental Subsidies and Related Items 15

Chapter 5. Loans and Other Receipts Balanced by
        Offsetting Obligations 16
Section 1. Loans 16
Section 2. Claim of Right Doctrine...16
Section 3. Illegal Income..16

Section 4. Deposits 17
Section 5. Conduit Situations 17

Chapter 6. Income From the Disposition of Property 18
Section 1. Introduction 18
Section 2. Determining the Amount of Gain..18
    A. Sales of Property and Transfers of Property in Satisfaction of a Claim.......18
    B. Basis of Property Received in an Exchange....................................19
    C. The Role of Debt in Amount Realized and Basis.........................20
Section 3. Complex Aspects of Realization 20
Section 4. Exclusion of Gains from the Sale of a Principal Residence 22

Chapter 7. The Relationship of Basis to Income Recognition 23
Section 1. Gifts of Property: Transferred Basis 23
Section 2. Transfers at Death: Fair Market Value Basis 24
Section 3. Gifts and Inheritance of Split Interests..24
Section 4. Income in Respect of a Decedent...25
Section 5. Tax Policy Aspects of Gratuitous Transfers of
       Appreciated Property 25
Section 6. Nonshareholder Contributions to Capital.......................................25

Chapter 8. Taxation of Periodic Income From Capital 27
Section 2. Tax Deferred and Tax-Exempt Investment Accounts........................27
Section 3. Special Treatment of Corporate Dividends 27
Section 4. Tax-Exempt Interest on State and Local Bonds 28
Section 5. Treatment of the Owner of Annuity and Life Insurance Contracts 28

Chapter 9. Damage Awards and Settlements and Insurance Recoveries ... 30
Section 1. Damages Received on Account of Property and Lost Profits..............30
Section 2. Damage Awards for Personal Injury...30
Section 3. Insurance Recoveries 31

Chapter 10. Income From the Cancellation of Indebtedness 33
Section 1. General Principles 33
Section 2. Statutory Codification of Cancellation of Indebtedness Rules 33
Section 3. The Disputed Debt, or Contested Liability Doctrine...........................35
Section 4. Cancellation of Indebtedness as a Medium of Payment 35

Chapter 11. Tax Expenditures...37
Section 1. The Concept of Tax Expenditures 37

PART III BUSINESS DEDUCTIONS AND CREDITS 38

**Chapter 12. Ordinary and Necessary Business and
Profit-Seeking Expenses 38**
Section 1. The Relevance of "Trade or Business" Versus "Profit-Seeking"
       Expenses 38
Section 2. The "Ordinary and Necessary" Limitation 39

Section 3. The Limitation of "Unreasonable" Compensation.................................39
Section 4. Expenses Related to Tax-Exempt Income 40
Section 5. "Public Policy" Limitations: Tax Penalties 40

Chapter 13. Deductible Profit-Seeking Expenses Versus Nondeductible Capital Expenditures..42
Section 2. Expenditures to Acquire or Produce Tangible Property 42
Section 3. Amounts Paid to Improve Tangible Property...43
Section 4. Costs to Acquire or Create Intangibles...44
Section 5. Business Investigations, Start-Up and Expansion Costs 44

Chapter 14. Cost Recovery Mechanisms..47
Section 1. Depreciation..47
    A. Accelerated Cost Recovery System..47
    B. Election to Expense Certain Depreciable Business Assets..........................47
Section 2. Statutory Amortization of Intangible Assets 48
Section 3. Expensing and Amortization Provisions..49
Section 4. Capital Recovery for Natural Resources..49

Chapter 15. Transactional Losses 50
Section 1. Business or Profit Seeking Losses 50
Section 2. Loss Disallowance Rules..51
Section 3. Bad Debts..52

Chapter 16. Interest as a Profit-Seeking Expense......................................53
Section 1. What is Interest?...53
Section 3. Limitations on the Interest Deduction 53

Chapter 17. Business Tax Credits 55

PART IV DUAL PURPOSE EXPENSES...56

Chapter 18. Determining When a Taxpayer is Engaging in a Business or Profit-Seeking Activity 56
Section 1. Is There a Profit-Seeking Motive? 56
Section 2. Business Use of Residence...58

Chapter 19. Expenses Involving Both Personal and Business Purposes 60
Section 1. General Principles 60
Section 2. Travel and Related Expenses...60
Section 3. Business Meals and Entertainment..62
Section 4. Statutory Limitations on Deductions for Certain Property...................63
Section 5. Clothing..64
Section 6. Child and Dependent Care 64

Chapter 20. Expenditures Involving Both Personal and Capital Aspects ...65
Section 1. Legal Expenses 65
Section 2. Expenses for Education and Seeking Employment 65

PART V DEDUCTIONS AND CREDITS FOR PERSONAL LIVING EXPENSES.. 67

Chapter 21. Itemized Personal Deductions................................... 67
Section 2. Medical Expenses 67
Section 3. Charitable Contributions 69
Section 4. State and Local Taxes 70
Section 5. Qualified Home Mortgage Interest 71
Section 6. Casualty Losses 71
Section 7. Limitations on Itemized Deductions..................................72

Chapter 22. Standard Deduction, Personal and Dependency Exemptions, and Personal Credits.. 73
Section 1. Personal Exemptions and the Standard Deduction.............73
Section 2. Personal Credits..76

Chapter 23. Tax Expenditures for Education 78

PART IV CHARACTERIZATION OF GAINS AND LOSSES............... 79

Chapter 24. Capital Gains and Losses 79
Section 1. Special Treatment of Capital Gains and Losses 79
Section 2. Definition of "Capital Asset" 80
   A. The Statutory Exclusions..80
      (1) Investment Property Versus Property Held For Sale to Customers 80
      (2) Section 1221(a)(2): Real Property and Depreciable Property Held For Use In The Taxpayer's Trade or Business 82
      (3) Section 1221(a)(3): Investment Profits Versus Reward For Personal Services...82
      (7) Section 1221(a)(7): Hedging Transactions 83
      (8) Section 1221(a)(8): Non-Inventory Supplies 84
   B. Judicial Limitations on Capital Asset Classification.......................84
Section 3. Sale or Exchange Requirement 85
   A. Termination of Taxpayer's Interest Without a "Transfer"— The Creditor's Situation..85
Section 4. Holding Period Requirement..86
Section 5. Special Statutory Treatment of Particular Gains and Losses.................87
Section 6. Transactional Problems of Capital Gains and Losses 87

Chapter 25. Sales of Assets Held for Use in a Trade or Business 89
Section 1. Section 1231 Property..89
Section 2. Sale of an Entire Business..92

PART VII DEFERRED RECOGNITION OF GAIN FROM PROPERTY 94

Chapter 26. Like-Kind Exchanges 94
Section 1. Like-Kind Exchanges in General 94
Section 2. Multiparty and Deferred Exchanges 96

Chapter 27. Involuntary Conversions and Other Deferred Recognition Transactions 99
Section 1. Involuntary Conversions 99

PART VIII TIMING OF INCOME AND DEDUCTIONS 101

Chapter 28. Tax Accounting Methods 101
Section 2. The Cash Method 101
Section 3. The Accrual Method 102
   A. Income Items 102
   B. Deduction Items 104
Section 4. Inventory Accounting 106

Chapter 29. The Annual Accounting Concept 107
Section 1. Transactional Problems 107
   B. Initial Deduction Followed by Later Recovery: The Tax Benefit Doctrine 107
   C. Initial Inclusion in Income Followed by Later Repayment 108
Section 2. Net Operating Loss Carryover and Carryback 108

Chapter 30. Deferred Compensation Arrangements 110
Section 1. Nonqualified Deferred Compensation Contracts 110
Section 2. Transfers of Property for Services 111

Chapter 31. Deferred Payment Sales 113
Section 1. Nonstatutory Deferred Reporting of Gains 113
Section 2. Installment Reporting Under Section 453 113

Chapter 32. Interest on Discount Obligations 116
Section 2. Original Issue Discount 116
Section 3. Bond Premium 118

PART IX TAX MOTIVATED TRANSACTIONS 119

Chapter 33 Transactions Involving Leased Property 119

Chapter 34. Nonrecourse Debt and Leveraged Tax Shelters 122
Section 1. Acquisition and Disposition of Property Subject to Nonrecourse Debt 122
Section 3. The Valuation of Property Subject to Debt 123

Chapter 35. Statutory Limitations on Leveraged Tax Shelters 125
Section 1. The At-Risk Limitation 125

Section 2. Passive Activity Loss Limitation 126

Chapter 36. Economic Substance Doctrine **129**

PART X THE TAXABLE UNIT **130**

Chapter 37. Shifting Income Among Taxable Units...............................**130**
Section 1. Income From Personal Services 130
Section 2. Income From Property...132
Section 3. Property That is the Product of Personal Efforts....................133
Section 4. Below-Market and Interest-Free Loans 133

Chapter 38. Taxation of Families...**135**
Section 1. The Married Couple as the Unit of Taxation..........................135
Section 2. Taxation of Children as Part of the Family Unit....................135
Section 3. Tax Aspects of Divorce and Separation 136
Section 4. Grantor Trusts 137

PART XI ALTERNATIVE MINIMUM TAX **139**

Chapter 39. Alternative Minimum Tax for Individuals...........................**139**

UNIVERSITY CASEBOOK SERIES®

DISCUSSION PROBLEMS FOR

FEDERAL INCOME TAXATION

SEVENTH EDITION

PART I

Introduction To Federal Income Taxation

CHAPTER 1

Introduction

SECTION 1. AN OVERVIEW OF POLICY ISSUES AND THE CURRENT INCOME TAX

A. SELECTION OF A TAX—GOALS AND CRITERIA

1. Tax systems are said to be evaluated on three primary criteria: equity, efficiency and simplicity.

   (a) Is it possible for all three criteria to be satisfied simultaneously?

   (b) If one criterion must yield to another, which should trump the others?

(c) If a tax system cannot be easily administered, can it be equitable or efficient?

B. THE STRUCTURE OF THE INCOME TAX AND SELECTED POLICY ISSUES

1. Under the Haig-Simons definition of income, is consumption part of the tax base (that is to say, are amounts spent on consumption subject to tax)? Why?

2. What, if any, is the difference between a tax system grounded in the Haig-Simons definition of income and one that explicitly but exclusively taxes consumption?

3. As you will see, the current tax system is actually a hybrid income/consumption system because it contains provisions that give it features of each. If you lived in an ideal world where pure systems could be enacted and could endure, which type would you support: income or consumption? Why?

4. In a system that defines the tax base as taxable income, if a single individual who has $100,000 of taxable income pays $30,000 of tax (an effective rate of 30 percent), how much should a single individual with $200,000 of taxable income pay? How about one with $400,000 of taxable income? $800,000? How about one with $50,000 of taxable income? How about one with $10,000 of taxable income?

5. If a country opts for a system of consumption taxes, must it jettison all attempts at progressivity?

SECTION 2. THE ROAD TO THE SIXTEENTH AMENDMENT AND THE MODERN FEDERAL INCOME TAX

1. Why was the 1894 income tax held to be unconstitutional?

SECTION 3. THE FEDERAL INCOME TAX SYSTEM AND THE MODERN FEDERAL INCOME TAX

A. THE LEGISLATIVE PROCESS

1. The President is upset about the state of the tax law. He asks you to write a speech that denounces the complexity of the "IRS Code" and in which he

promises to use his executive power to prevent the IRS from burying taxpayers with forms that they cannot understand and that they need to hire an expert to complete. Before agreeing to write any such speech, what should you tell the President?

2. Senator Susan Anthony wants to add a provision to the Internal Revenue Code to provide a deduction for amounts spent to purchase non-prescription contraceptives. May she begin by introducing such a provision on the floor of the Senate? Even assuming a majority of her fellow senators agree, what must happen before the provision can become law?

B. THE ADMINISTRATIVE PROCESS

1. Caroline has just received a Notice of Deficiency from the Internal Revenue Service and has hired you to represent her. Although her accountant represented her through the Service's administrative process, she now feels that retaining someone trained in the adversary system is necessary. Caroline insists that she owes no tax and preliminarily you agree with her. What factors will influence your decision on whether to advise her to pursue her case in the Tax Court, a Federal District Court, or the Court of Federal Claims?

C. THE JUDICIAL PROCESS

1. You represent a client from state in which you are attending school in a case before the Tax Court. Courts of Appeal for the Seventh and Third Circuits have issued conflicting opinions on the issue. What law will the Tax Court apply to your case?

E. THE TAX ADVISER

1. You represent Caroline in her acquisition of a condominium from a developer. Tax issues have been prominent in the negotiations. In reviewing the draft of the final agreement, you realize that the tax lawyer for the developer has overlooked the adverse impact on his client of a highly technical Code provision. You have worked with that tax lawyer on several prior transactions and expect to do so in the future. Can or should you alert the other tax lawyer to his mistake?

2.Your expertise in real estate law grows and you become a well-known figure in Washington circles. In the course of your work, you have discovered numerous provisions that clever tax lawyers can exploit to reduce income taxes nearly to zero. The House Ways and Means Committee plans to hold hearings on the reform of the income tax treatment of real estate. The Committee Staff has asked you to testify so that the Committee members can understand how current rules are being exploited by those in the real estate business. Can or should you testify, utilizing the knowledge you have gained over the years as the basis for your testimony?

PART II

GROSS INCOME

CHAPTER 2

GENERAL PRINCIPLES OF GROSS INCOME

SECTION 1. INCOME

A. INCREASE IN NET WORTH

1. Ulysses found a $100-dollar bill in the middle of the sidewalk. He picked it up and put it in his pocket. Does Ulysses realize gross income as a result?

2. While shopping at a flea market, Phoebe bought a jewelry box for $20. At home, she discovered the box contained an emerald ring. A local jeweler appraised the ring at $1,000. Does Phoebe realize any gross income as a result of these events?

3. (a) As an archeology professor at Marshall College, Henry Jones, Jr. receives many complimentary textbooks, maps, and models from publishers who hope

he will use their products in his courses. Are these items gross income to Henry?

(b) What if Henry gave one of the books, valued at $100, to Marion as a birthday gift? What if Henry donated the other books to charity and claimed a deduction?

4. When Joey stopped by the local coffee shop recently, he was the lucky one-millionth customer to walk through the door. The coffee shop owner gave Joey his choice of $1,000 cash or a cappuccino machine (which cost the coffee shop $1,000). The coffee shop usually sells that model for $1,750, but that week it was on sale for $1,500. However, that precise model normally retails for $2,000 elsewhere. If Joey wanted to sell the machine, he could get $1,250 at the local pawnshop. In the end, Joey decides to accept the cappuccino machine. How much gross income must he recognize?

B. INDIRECT RECEIPTS

1. Evil Empire Corporation, in addition to running a successful and well-funded baseball team, owns a factory that produces sports apparel. The CEO, Stein, and the CFO, Brenner, with board approval, decided that it would be cost efficient not to install the required filter technology on the factory's smokestacks, since the omission would probably not be detected. However, Evil Empire was caught and the state of New York commenced criminal action against Evil Empire, Stein, Brenner, and all seven of the directors. All of the defendants pled *nolo contendere*. Evil Empire paid the fines, totaling $500,000, that were levied against the company, including $25,000 in fines levied against each of the defendant-employees and directors. Should Stein, Brenner, and the directors recognize any gross income?

2. Dizzy Entertainment Corp., which operates a chain of the world's most popular amusement parks, has agreed to pay its CEO, Mickey, a salary of $3 million net of federal income taxes. Assuming that Mickey has sufficient income from other sources and that all of his salary would be taxed at the top rate of 35 percent, what must his salary be next year so that he will have $3 million after federal income taxes?

SECTION 2. THE REALIZATION REQUIREMENT

1. Joan purchased a jewelry box at a flea market for $20. She took the box to Antiques Roadshow and discovered that the box was actually worth $5,000. Does Joan realize any gross income? When? How much?

2. Deciding she is on a lucky streak, Joan decides again to visit the flea market. Before leaving, she decides to buy a few picture frames (at a total cost of $50) so that she may hang some photographs in her foyer. Celeste falls in love with the frames and offers Joan $250. Joan considers three possibilities. She could refuse to sell the frames, and use them to hang the photographs. She could sell the frames to Celeste for $250. Or she could trade the frames to Celeste in exchange for being allowed to eat five free meals in Celeste's restaurant. Would any of these actions be realization events?

3. (a) Cartools, Inc. has 400,000 shares of stock outstanding. Half of the shares are owned by Tim, who paid $10 per share for them and the other half are owned by Al, who also paid $10 per share for them. Cartools, Inc. has had a very good year and Tim and Al decide that it would be good to move those earnings from earned surplus to stated capital. To accomplish that, they cause Cartools to declare a stock dividend of a half share for each existing share – in other words, Tim and Al now own 300,000 shares each. Have either Tim or Al realized gross income?

   (b) Does your answer change if Cartools gave Tim and Al a choice of taking the stock dividend or taking cash equal to the fair market value of the 100,000 shares that would have been paid as a dividend?

SECTION 3. IMPUTED INCOME

1. (a) Carla Frugal has saved $500,000 which she has invested in interest bearing instruments that pay her $2,000 per month. After paying tax on the interest, Carla is able to pay the rent on a modest apartment. Jack Grasshopper also has accumulated $500,000 that he uses to purchase a very nice home. Should the income tax cause the value of living in the home to be included in Jack's income? Is the exclusion of imputed rental income unfairly discriminatory against those who rent rather than own homes? Does it matter that everyone is free to rent or own?

   (b) Would the efficiency or equity of the tax system be improved by including in income the imputed income from owner occupied housing?

2. Danica owns an expensive car. Should she be taxed on the imputed rental value of the vehicle? What about the rental value of items Danica purchases for her home, such as furniture, the dishwasher and the lawnmower? Where should the inclusion of the imputed rental value of property stop, and why?

3. Clarice decides to move her accounts to Local Bank. A representative tells her that the bank normally charges $3 for ATM withdrawals, a $10 general

monthly service charge, $.50 every time a customer checks her balance online, and $15 for electronic bill payments. However, these charges are waived for customers who maintain a $2,000 minimum balance. If Clarice maintains the minimum balance, must she include the value of these services in her gross income?

4. Dana and her husband Michael are not happy with the local school system – public or private. They decide that Michael will quit his accounting job and stay at home to "home-school" their two children, thus foregoing his $100,000 annual salary. Private schools in the area cost $15,000 per year and the couple is in the 35 percent marginal tax bracket. How should this affect their decision?

CHAPTER 3

COMPENSATION FOR SERVICES

SECTION 1. NONCASH ECONOMIC GAINS

1. After many years of public service in the New York City District Attorney's Office, Jack moved into private practice. His first client was his old friend Lenny, who was accused of breaking and entering. As a result of Jack's skillful efforts, Lenny was acquitted. Grateful, yet cash strapped and unable to pay the fee, Lenny offered Jack the chance to use his upstate hunting cabin for three weeks. Jack accepted, and enjoyed a short vacation at Lenny's cabin (which usually rents for $450/week). Has Jack realized gross income as a result of this transaction? What about Lenny?

2. When Jack returned, he found that his partner, Carmichael, had been charged with possessing marijuana. Jack successfully defended Carmichael. The pair made no attempt to account for this work in the division of the partnership's profits, even though Jack's services would have cost any other client $3,000. Has Jack realized gross income from these events? What about Carmichael?

3. While Jack was on vacation, as a favor his old friend Van Buren agreed to cut his lawn, pick up his mail and check on his house each week.. Later, Van Buren went on vacation, so Jack agreed to return the favor. However, after mowing the yard once, Jack realized that yard work was not as glamorous as making a closing argument to a jury. Therefore, Jack decided to pay a teenager, who lived next door, $100 to cut Van Buren's grass in each of the final two weeks. Have Jack and Van Buren realized gross income as a result of these events?

8. (a) Gill manages the Temptation Island Resort Hotel, which features a beachfront hotel and a number of separate bungalows. Gill, his wife, Mary Ann, and their children live in a bungalow on the edge of the hotel property. Gill buys groceries from local stores and directly from some farmers, all on credit accounts that are paid by the hotel. Gill is on-call any time of the day or night and is required to live on the hotel premises so that he is easily accessible to answer any calls. Would Gill be correct in excluding value of the groceries and the use of the bungalow from his gross income?

(b) Would your answer change if Gill was allowed to live in a four-bedroom bungalow because he was married and had children, but would have been given only a one-bedroom bungalow if he had been single?

Section 2. Employee Fringe Benefits

A. Statutory Exclusions Based on Tax Policy and Administrative Convenience

1. Northworst Airlines allows its employees to travel on its airplanes for free, as long as there is space available. Employees must be present at the gate at least 45 minutes before departure and will be allowed on the airplane once all ticketed and standby passengers have boarded.

   (a) Amelia, a flight attendant, goes to the gate for a flight bound for Honolulu and is permitted onto the aircraft pursuant to the foregoing procedure. She is seated in a first class seat that normally sells for $5,000. Does Amelia realize gross income? Why or why not?

   (b) Does your answer change if Amelia consumes food and drink while on the plane and enjoys being waited on by the flight attendants?

   (c) Instead of Amelia, assume that Amelia's spouse, Viktor, follows the procedure described above and takes the flight to Honolulu. Is there a different result? Why or why not?

   (d) Amelia is unmarried but has a domestic partner who follows the procedure described above and takes the flight to Honolulu. Is there a different result? Why or why not?

   (e) Instead of Amelia, assume that Amelia's mother follows the procedure described above and takes the flight to Honolulu. Is there a different result? Why or why not?

2. Northworst Airlines has modified the policy described in Problem 1 above: only employees who hold the rank of vice president or above may avail themselves of the opportunity to fly free. Employees at the rank of vice president or above make up only 1 percent of all of the airline's employees and they are the most highly compensated employees of the airline. Marshall, vice-president for operations of the airline, follows the procedure described above and takes the trip to Honolulu. Will he realize gross income? Why or why not?

3. Brittany works for a hotel chain that allows its employees and their immediate family members to stay for free in any of its facilities as long as there is an empty room. Brittany's mother is allowed to stay for free in one of the hotel's rooms while on vacation (the room was empty, but would normally have cost $200 per night). Does either Brittany or her mother realize gross income from this event? Why or why not?

4. (a) European Car Sales sells BMW automobiles. Damian, a salesperson, was allowed to purchase a new BMW for $35,000, even though that model usually sells for $40,000. During the year, European Car Sales sold 200 automobiles for an aggregate price of $8 million and paid $6.8 million for those automobiles. How much gross income must Damian recognize?

(b) Would your answer change if European Car Sales had paid $7.2 million for the automobiles?

B. EMPLOYEE BENEFITS EXCLUDED FROM GROSS INCOME TO FURTHER SOCIAL POLICY GOALS

1. Liz's employer paid $3,000 of medical insurance premiums last year for a family medical insurance policy for Liz. The employer provides the same benefits to all employees. Liz's daughter Carrie was hospitalized and the insurance company paid $10,000 directly to the medical provider. Must Liz include either or both the medical insurance premiums and proceeds in her gross income?

2. (a) The architectural firm of Wright, Lloyd & Frank is operated as a professional corporation. It only provides medical insurance to its four senior architects, who own all of the stock of the corporation. The firm also employs six junior architects, six drafters, and six administrative assistants. Last year the firm paid $2,800 of medical insurance premiums for each of the senior architects, but did not provide any medical coverage for junior architects or for any of the other employees. How much gross income, if any, do the senior architects have as a result of the insurance coverage?

(b) The firm also provides for uninsured reimbursement of dental expenses for all senior architects. Wright was reimbursed for $3,000 of dental expenses, and Lloyd was reimbursed $1,500. Must either recognize any gross income?

CHAPTER 4

GIFTS, INHERITANCES AND SIMILAR ITEMS

SECTION 1. GIFTS AND INHERITANCES

1. Every year during the month of December Dr. Cliff Hanger of the Community Hospital receives many gifts from patients who are grateful for the care he has given them and the sense of humor with which he delivers it. The gifts include such things as bottles of wine, hams, books, and flowers. Although he rarely receives any gift worth more than $50, the total value of the gifts usually amounts to nearly $1,000. Does Dr. Hanger realize gross income as a result of receiving these items?

2. When Dr. Hanger decided to retire from the practice of medicine, the staff at Community Hospital took up a collection to purchase season tickets to the Philadelphia 76ers, and a convertible, so that he could travel to the games in style, as retirement gifts. When the staff came up $1,000 short, they convinced Community Hospital's administration to contribute the final amount. Does Dr. Hanger realize gross income on the receipt of the season tickets and convertible?

3. (a) Once Dr. Hanger no longer had to get up in the middle of the night to deliver babies, he decided to open a clinic in North Philadelphia. His clinic grew rapidly and he wanted to make certain that it would continue to do so even if he decided to hang up his stethoscope and retire for good. To that end, he hired his cousin's daughter, Jing-Mei, who recently completed a family practice residency in Chicago. Dr. Hanger promised Jing-Mei that if she came to Philadelphia and joined the clinic, he would include in his will a provision to pay off her medical school loans. When Dr. Hanger's executor pays off Jing-Mei's outstanding educational loans, are the payments gross income to Jing-Mei?

(b) Does your answer to Part (a) above depend on whether Jing-Mei receives a fair market value wage during the time that she works in the clinic? What if Jing-Mei had wanted to work in a clinic but had trouble securing such a job because she was a certified plastic surgeon and prospective employers thought she would only be with them for a short while and then return to the lucrative practice she had left behind?

4. Claire Counselor, a lawyer, always gives her assistant a birthday gift. Last year, she gave her assistant a $100 bill. This year, Claire gave her assistant a $100 gift certificate to a hot new restaurant. Next year Claire is considering giving her assistant a $100 bottle of wine. Does Claire's assistant realize gross income as a result of receiving these items?

5. Claire disapproves of her assistant's fiancé, whom she suspects of physically abusing her assistant. Claire is considering offering the fiancé $10,000 to break off the engagement. Would accepting the offer affect the fiancé's gross income? How would your answer change if Claire gave her assistant $10,000 to break off the engagement?

6. (a) Consider restaurant tips. What is the argument that tips should be considered gifts? What if a customer leaves a 75 percent tip?

(b) Should the IRS make underreported tips a priority? Why or why not?

SECTION 2. LIFE INSURANCE DEATH BENEFITS

1. (a) Sam was shot and killed during a robbery at his bar. His wife, Diane, was the beneficiary of his $200,000 whole life insurance policy. Diane collected the $200,000 face value of the policy from the insurance company. Does she realize gross income from this transaction?

(b) Instead, suppose Diane exercises an option in the policy to receive interest payments on the $200,000 for the remainder of her life (an amount estimated to be $10,000 annually), with the $200,000 principal of the policy to be paid to her daughter upon Diane's death. Must the daughter include the $200,000 principal in her income?

(c) What if Diane elects to receive an annuity of $14,000 a year? Assume her life expectancy is 20 years and there is no refund if Diane dies before receiving full payment.

2. Becket suffers from a terminal disease and has roughly a year to live. He has a life insurance policy worth $400,000; the policy also offers accelerated payments to those who qualify. Based on his medical condition and short projected life span, Becket qualifies. If he decides to take the accelerated payment option, and receive approximately $350,000 to pay for his medical expenses, will this be included in his gross income?

3. After Niles died, his employer paid his estate $2,000 of salary still owed to Niles. The board of directors of Niles' employer also decided to give his widow Daphne the $10,000 it expected to give to Niles as a year-end bonus, as well as an additional $5,000. Are these three payments gross income to the recipients?

SECTION 3. PRIZES

1. Carol was the winner of the latest game show spin-off. She won a two-week trip to Bermuda (including all transportation, food, and lodging for Carol and four friends). The trip was non-transferable and was required to be used within one year. Carol took her husband and three children. Such a trip typically costs $5,000, but the airline and hotel usually give families a discount of $300 and $200, respectively. How does this transaction affect Carol's gross income? What if Carol and her family really value the trip at only $2,000 because they would not have paid more than that to take it?

2.For his required third year seminar paper at Newest University Law Factory, Ronald McLawyer argued for a complete overhaul of the federal income tax system. His tax professor was so impressed with the paper that he submitted it to the American Tax Policy Institute's Tannenwald Writing Competition, which does not accept direct submissions directly from students but rather requires that submissions be sponsored by an academic or member of the Institute. Ronald won $5,000 in cash and the opportunity to have his paper published. How much gross income must Ronald recognize as a result of receiving the $5,000?

SECTION 4. SCHOLARSHIPS

1. Sheri Scholar is a graduate student at the Marine Institute of Technology where she is a Ph.D. candidate in biological oceanography. Her tuition is $35,000 per year. Sheri has a $40,000 scholarship from MIT. She is required to teach a freshman biology course as a condition of the scholarship. Other lecturers who are not students of the university are paid $7,000 to teach the same course. How much, if any, of Sheri's scholarship is includible in gross income?

2. Clarence is a student at Famous Law School. FLS is known for its championship moot court team. Clarence was offered a full scholarship to FLS, covering his tuition, books, and room and board. The scholarship is renewable annually provided Clarence maintains a B+ average and continues

to participate on the FLS moot court team. Is his scholarship excludable from gross income?

3. Erika, the most recent Miss America winner, was accepted to Enormous State University School of Veterinary Medicine. Part of her award for winning was a $15,000 scholarship to the school of her choice to cover tuition, books, room, and board. This scholarship will be doubled if the winner postpones school for one year, and instead travels the world, promoting the pageant. Erika decided to take the additional scholarship money, as well as the opportunity to travel the world, and she waited one year before attending ESU. When she does begin school and receives the benefit of the $30,000 scholarship, how much must she include in income?

SECTION 5. GOVERNMENTAL SUBSIDIES AND RELATED ITEMS

1. Jordan, single and retired, has two sources of income. First, he draws a $20,000 annual pension. Second, he receives $10,000 a year in social security. However, Jordan is looking for a new challenge and a chance to interact with other people. He is considering working as a part-time basketball coach at the local community college. The job would pay $9,000 a year. How would this affect Jordan's gross income?

CHAPTER 5

LOANS AND OTHER RECEIPTS BALANCED BY OFFSETTING OBLIGATIONS

SECTION 1. LOANS

1. Jamal, a computer science major, dropped out of school to start an unincorporated software company. To finance development of new software, Jamal borrowed $1,500,000 from Keeping Our Fingers Crossed Venture Capital Fund. In exchange for the money Jamal gave the Fund a nonrecourse promissory note, due in ten years and secured by a 50 percent interest in the software that Jamal eventually develops and copyrights. The interest on the loan is prime plus 3 percent. Is this a true loan? If not, what is it?

SECTION 2. CLAIM OF RIGHT DOCTRINE

1. Gordon owns 85 percent of the stock of Performance Motor Parts Mfg. Corp. Last year he earned a salary of $350,000 and a $700,000 bonus. Gordon's written employment contract requires him to repay any portion of the bonus that the IRS, in an audit, determines should be classified as a dividend rather than as compensation. This year, the IRS audited the company. The IRS determined that a portion of the putative bonus, $450,000, was actually a dividend. Pursuant to the terms of his contract, Gordon repaid that amount to the company. Should Gordon amend his last year's tax return to report only $600,000 of income, or should he deduct the $450,000 repayment this year?

SECTION 3. ILLEGAL INCOME

1. Arthur previously sold tax shelter investments for an accounting firm that is no longer in business. After leaving that firm, Arthur created a new investment plan known as "From Rags to Riches Painlessly." Under the program, Arthur's clients entrusted their money to him, thinking that the money would be invested on their behalf. Arthur guaranteed his investors a return of 5 percentage points over the yield of Treasury bills and told them they could

withdraw the money at any time. Arthur said that the program was far too complex to explain, so he did not provide his clients with any information on how the funds were invested. Last year, Arthur received $3,000,000 from investors. He never maintained any structured plan, although he did use half of the money to purchase T-bills in his own name. He used $450,000 to pay the "yield" to his investors and used $150,000 to repay investors who chose to withdraw. The remaining $900,000 was used to purchase a mansion in the Chicago suburbs and otherwise maintain Arthur's lifestyle. How much of the $3,000,000 must be included in Arthur's gross income?

SECTION 4. DEPOSITS

1. (a) Jimbob Meyers is the proprietor of the Polo Horse Bar and Grill, which recently relocated to the Bakersfield Mall. Jimbob paid Oilcap Industries, the owner of the mall, a $20,000 security deposit, which was the equivalent of one-month's rent. Under the terms of the lease, Oilcap must return the deposit at the end of the lease term, less any amount retained to repair damages caused by Jimbob's occupancy. In the meantime, Oilcap may retain the security deposit, which it commingled with its own funds. Oilcap is not obligated to pay interest on the deposit. Is Oilcap required to include the deposit in gross income?

(b) Would your answer to (a) change if the deposit were forfeitable to secure payment of rent under the lease?

SECTION 5. CONDUIT SITUATIONS

1. Mary Jane makes a living growing and selling marijuana. The state legislature is considering legalizing the growth of marijuana for personal use. Mary Jane is concerned that the initiative will destroy her lucrative livelihood. Therefore, she goes around the state giving speeches on the evils of drug use and convinces many people to contribute to her fictional organization "People for Mary Jane But Against Marijuana." She collects $300,000 in donations and deposits that amount in a bank account under the name of her fake organization. Of the total $300,000, Mary Jane used $270,000 to advertise the campaign. After the voters rejected the initiative, Mary Jane used the remaining $30,000 to buy supplies to expand her marijuana business. How much must Mary Jane include in her gross income?

CHAPTER 6

INCOME FROM THE DISPOSITION OF PROPERTY

SECTION 1. INTRODUCTION

1. George owns the baseball that dribbled through Bill Buckner's legs and helped the Mets win the 1986 World Series. George purchased the ball last year for $10,000. Unfortunately, George is now in need of cash, so he has decided to sell the ball to Jerry for $15,000. Actually, George is so desperate for cash that he would sell the ball for anything over $5,000, but he was able to negotiate the higher price with Jerry. Secretly, Jerry is thrilled with the price – he considers it low, because he was willing to spend up to $20,000. Unbeknownst to each, any memorabilia store owner in the city would be willing to buy the ball for $25,000. On average, Major League Baseball buys its baseballs, which cost roughly $3 to produce, for $5 each. What gain does George realize? Is there a better possible measure of George's gain?

SECTION 2. DETERMINING THE AMOUNT OF GAIN

A. SALES OF PROPERTY AND TRANSFERS OF PROPERTY IN SATISFACTION OF A CLAIM

1. To start Vandelay Industries, several years ago George borrowed $10,000 from Cosmo. This month, Cosmo demanded repayment. George is a little short on cash, so he offered to pay Cosmo by transferring to him a tiny plot of land he owns in the Hamptons. George had purchased the plot a number of years ago for $6,000, but it is now worth $10,000. Cosmo agreed and George deeded the land to him. What are the tax consequences to George and Cosmo?

2. Ticky-Tacky Homes, Inc is in the business of developing housing subdivisions. The company is considering selling its top salesman a home in one of its subdivisions for $70,000. The home cost $60,000 to build and normally sells for $100,000. How much gross income, if any, must Ticky-Tacky realize as a result of this transaction?

18

3. Jay owns 50 shares of stock in NBC Inc. Jay's 50 shares have a total basis of $1,000 and a fair market value of $50,000. Dave owns 100 shares of CBS, which have a total basis of $10,000 and a fair market value of $50,000. If Jay and Dave trade all of their shares to one another, how much gain must each recognize?

4. Pat is a real estate developer. A few years ago, Pat purchased Elysian Fields Farm for $1,100,000. The property included 120 acres of undeveloped land on which there was a small lake plus three acres that included a beautiful farmhouse and a few barns. At first, Pat had only been interested in the undeveloped land. However, rather than sell the 120 acres of undeveloped land to Pat for $800,000, the original owner was only interested in selling the entire estate, for $1,100,000. Pat quickly agreed to the counterproposal and after the deal had closed, Pat immediately went to work improving Elysian Fields. Pat obtained approval to subdivide the land into 60 two-acre plots and the three-acre farmhouse lot. Pat was quickly able to sell the three-acre farmhouse lot for $300,000. So far, Pat has sold all ten 2-acre lots with lake frontage for $150,000 each and ten of the other fifty 2-acre lots for $30,000 each. How much gain has Pat realized?

5. Alan does not trust the stock market and very seldom invests in it. However, a few years ago, Alan purchased 100 shares of Specific Motors Corporation for $1,000. A year later, he purchased an additional 100 shares of Specific Motors Corporation for $2,000. Recently, Alan has become uncomfortable having so much money invested in the market. He decides to sell 100 shares of Specific Motors, which is currently trading at $15 a share. Has Alan realized a $500 loss or a $500 gain?

B. Basis of Property Received in an Exchange

1. Jerry owns the cuff links of a famous comedian. He purchased them two years ago for $10,000, but they are now worth $16,000. Cosmo owns a rare Superman comic worth $14,000 that he originally purchased for $6,000. While the two friends realize the fair market values of their properties are unequal, their own subjective valuations make a trade worthwhile to each. If they do agree to trade the two items, how much gain must Jerry and Cosmo each recognize? After the trade, what is Cosmo's basis for the cuff links? What is Jerry's basis for the comic book?

2. As interim CEO of Peterman Corporation, Elaine was allowed to purchase 10,000 shares of company stock for $100,000. At that time, the shares were trading for $40 a share, so the acquisition was actually worth $400,000. If

Elaine now sells her shares for a total of $600,000, how much gain must she recognize?

3. Rob Crusoe found an old Spanish gold doubloon on the beach that he had appraised at $7,000. If Rob later sells the doubloon for $10,000, what is his basis for computing gain or loss? What if he sells the doubloon for $5,000?

4. Mary Peter-Paul owned a parcel of land, Honah Lee Farm. Last December, when Honah Lee Farm was worth $80,000, Jackie Paper paid Mary $2,000 for an option to buy the land anytime during the next six months for $79,000. Jackie exercised the option in March, when the Honah Lee Farm had a fair market value of $92,000. What is Jackie's basis in Honah Lee Farm?

C. The Role of Debt in Amount Realized and Basis

1. Years ago, Beulah purchased a plot of land for $40,000 and constructed an apartment building on it at a cost of $760,000. All of these costs were paid by the proceeds of a loan from Usury Bank & Trust Co. secured by a mortgage on the property. Currently, the basis of the building is $680,000 (as a result of adjustments to basis for depreciation deductions, which will be discussed later in the course). The outstanding balance on the loan has been reduced to $700,000. Beulah sold the property to Clark for $250,000 in cash plus Clark's contractual promise to assume the mortgage. How much gain must Beulah recognize? What is Clark's basis in the property?

Section 3. Complex Aspects of Realization

1. In January, Allyson borrowed $75,000 from Last National Bank, using as security a mortgage on a downtown commercial building she owns and in which she had a $50,000 basis. It was a nonrecourse mortgage loan, and Allyson used the money to make an unrelated investment. Unfortunately for Allyson, a new shopping mall opened in July on the beltway, and many downtown stores, including those renting space in Allyson's building, have moved. Now Allyson is unable to rent many of her stores. Also, she has been unable to sell the building itself. She wants to sell the building for $75,000, but has only received one offer, for $50,000. Recently, the tax commissioner assessed the property at $60,000 for local real property tax purposes. What are the consequences of these events to Allyson?

2. Eventually, Allyson decided to move out to the beltway herself. Last National Bank loaned Allyson $2,000,000 to finance a shopping center. The interest rate was 10 percent, payable monthly. The principal was payable only on maturity

in 20 years. However, once again, Allyson's bad luck struck. Two years after the loan was made, the local economy took a dive, and Allyson lost several clients. Does Last National Bank realize a gain or loss with respect to the loan in either of the following situations?

(a) When Allyson became a month late on an interest payment, the Bank was entitled to declare the loan in default and invoke the acceleration clause (causing the principal to be due immediately). Giving Allyson and the economy the benefit of the doubt, the Bank waived this option.

(b) Allyson and the bank agreed to modify the loan by reducing the interest rate to 9 percent.

3. Carl owned 100 shares of Intel Corporation stock, which had a fair market value of $1,700 and a basis of $1,200. Denise owned 50 shares of stock in EDS Corporation which had a fair market value of $1,700 and a basis of $1,500. Carl exchanged his Intel stock with Denise for her EDS stock. How much gain must Carl and Denise recognize?

4. Emma owns 10,000 shares of Austen Inc. The shares are worth $2 million and have a basis of $100,000. Emma is interested in cashing out her investment, but wants to avoid taxation on her $1.9 million of gain. Her broker suggests a "short sale against the box." Under this plan, Emma would "borrow" 10,000 shares of Austen Inc. from her broker (using her own shares as security) and would sell the borrowed shares on the market for $2 million. Emma would then have $2 million in cash and she would have eliminated her risk, because her long term and short-term interests would offset each other. If the value of the stock she owns goes up, that increase will be offset by the increased amount it will cost her to replace the shares she borrowed from her broker, and vice versa. Will this plan work? That is, does the plan provide Emma the risk elimination benefits of a cash sale, without being treated as a realization event for tax purposes?

5. Newman, tired of the life of a civil servant, becomes a securities dealer. At the start of the year, his portfolio includes the following stocks (none of which are held for investment) – 10 shares of Kramerica ($5 per share basis), 20 shares of Play Now Inc. ($40 per share basis) and 20 shares of NBC ($100 per share basis). At the end of the year, Kramerica is trading for $11 a share, Play Now Inc. is trading for $20 a share, and NBC is trading for $120 a share. How much gain or loss does Newman realize with respect to his portfolio?

SECTION 4. EXCLUSION OF GAINS FROM THE SALE OF A PRINCIPAL RESIDENCE

1. Guy T. Helvering was a successful lawyer in Kansas. After a stint as mayor of Salina and State Highway Director in Kansas, he was appointed Commissioner of Internal Revenue. He owned a house in Salina, which he sold when he became Commissioner and moved to Washington, D.C. At that time, figuring that he would no longer have time for golf, Guy also sold a house he owned in Hilton Head, South Carolina, where he spent holidays and at least six weeks during the summer. Guy realized a gain of $200,000 on the Hilton Head house and $520,000 on his residence in Salina, Kansas.

   (a) If Guy is single, how much of the gain on the sale of the houses will be included in his income?

   (b) If Guy is married, and owned both homes jointly with his wife, how much of the gain will be included in the couple's gross income?

CHAPTER 7

THE RELATIONSHIP OF BASIS TO INCOME RECOGNITION

SECTION 1. GIFTS OF PROPERTY: TRANSFERRED BASIS

1. Juan gave his daughter Carla 1,000 shares of Xenon Corp stock, which he had originally purchased for $60,000. At the time of the transfer, the total fair market value of the stock was $80,000. How much gain or loss would Carla recognize if she sold the stock for:

   (a) $120,000?

   (b) $70,000?

   (c) $50,000?

2. If Juan's basis in the Xenon Corp stock in Problem 1 had been $100,000 and he had given it to Carla when it had a fair market value of $80,000, how much gain or loss would Carla recognize if she later sold the stock for:

   (a) $120,000?

   (b) $70,000?

   (c) $90,000?

3. (a) If Juan sold the stock in Problem 1, above, to Carla for $70,000 how much gain or loss would Juan recognize? What would Carla's basis in the stock be?

   (b) If Juan sold the stock in Problem 2, above, to Carla for $70,000 how much gain or loss would Juan recognize? What would Carla's basis in the stock bc?

SECTION 2. TRANSFERS AT DEATH: FAIR MARKET VALUE BASIS

1. Thirty years ago, Joss's Uncle Matt purchased 1,000 shares of Serenity Computers, Inc., an upstart technology company, for a total of $20,000, or $20 per share. Later, on his deathbed, Uncle Matt promised to transfer all of the shares to Joss. At that time, the stock was trading for $60 a share. A week later, Uncle Matt died, and Joss, as Matt's sole heir, inherited the stock, then trading for $80 a share. Now, a month later, Joss has decided to sell the stock for a total of $70,000. How much gain or loss does Joss recognize?

2. Several years ago, shortly after their marriage, Ian and Jenny purchased for $2,000,000 beachfront land held for speculative investment, title to which they took as joint tenants with rights of survivorship. Ian died last year and the land was appraised at $8,000,000 for inheritance and estate tax purposes. Jenny sold the land this year, and cleared $7,800,000 after paying the real estate broker's commission. How much gain or loss has Jenny realized and recognized?

3. The Shrubs are a married couple from Texas. Immensely wealthy from their company, Big Oil Inc., the Shrubs purchased a ranch for $4,000,000 many years ago. Unfortunately, Mr. Shrub recently choked to death on a pretzel. His will left everything to his wife, Mrs. Shrub. The ranch was appraised at $10,000,000. Mrs. Shrub decided it was too painful to hang onto the family ranch, so she sold it immediately for $10,000,000. How much gain or loss must Mrs. Shrub recognize? Is your answer affected by the fact that Texas is a community property state?

SECTION 3. GIFTS AND INHERITANCE OF SPLIT INTERESTS

1. Tom would like to give his good friend Dick a gift. He is considering two options. He might give Dick $10,000 a year for 10 years. Alternatively, Tom might give Dick a 50 percent interest in his rights to payments from his winning ticket from the LoneStar State Lottery (the winning ticket pays $20,000 per year for 10 years). From a tax perspective, which option would Dick prefer?

2. Grandma Shrub, has a fund of $100,000 that earns 10 percent per year. Purely from a federal income tax perspective, if the Court had accepted the taxpayer's argument in *Irwin v. Gavit*, would Grandma Shrub be better advised (assuming that one of her objectives is to minimize the tax burdens of the objects of her affection) to give the fund to her son George for life, with the remainder to his daughters, Barb and Jenna, or should she leave it to George outright?

SECTION 4. INCOME IN RESPECT OF A DECEDENT

1. Jezebel was the president and CEO of Ahab Whale Oil Inc. She was invaluable to Ahab Whale Oil, skillfully steering it through economic downturns and helping the company reach new heights in economic upturns. Jezebel earned $1,000,000 a year as well as a bonus, carefully tied to Ahab Whale Oil's economic performance. Jezebel died just before her annual bonus was to be announced. Actually, the compensation committee had already calculated the amount – $15,000,000 – and the only thing that remained was to hand Jezebel the check. Jezebel's husband, Ishmael, and their children had grown accustomed to her large bonuses and were not sure they could survive until the estate went through probate. Therefore, Ishmael, who inherited Jezebel's right to the bonus, sold the contractual claim to the bonus to Opportunistic Bank & Trust Co. for $14,000,000 pending distribution (which now would go to the bank, as assignee of the claim). Does Ishmael recognize gain or loss when he receives the $14,000,000 from the bank in exchange for his claim to the bonus? How much gain or loss does the bank recognize when it collects the $15,000,000?

SECTION 5. TAX POLICY ASPECTS OF GRATUITOUS TRANSFERS OF APPRECIATED PROPERTY

1. Assume you work on the staff of the Senate Finance Committee and have been asked to draft a proposal for reform of the taxation of transfers of property at death. Taking into account considerations of tax policy only, and ignoring (perhaps unrealistically), political considerations, which of the options discussed in Section 5 for handling disposition of property at death would you recommend – carryover basis, fair market value basis, or treating death as a realization event? Why?

SECTION 6. NONSHAREHOLDER CONTRIBUTIONS TO CAPITAL

1. (a) The Big Yellow Taxi Corporation provides bus service in the city of Paradise. The law firm of Sweat, Shop & Nochanceatpartner gives a large contribution to Big Yellow Taxi, so that its lawyers may ride for free. Will Big Yellow Taxi realize gross income as the result of this receipt?

(b) The law firm builds a private bridge that provides a short cut to Sweat's main office at a cost of $1,000,000. Because the law firm does not want to be responsible for upkeep of the bridge, it deeds the bridge to Big Yellow Taxi.

What are the tax implications of this transaction for Big Yellow Taxi? What is its basis in the bridge?

(c) Suppose that instead of the bridge, the law firm gives $50,000 to Big Yellow Taxi, but this time does not attach the requirement that its lawyers be able to ride for free. Indeed, there are no strings attached. Big Yellow Taxi uses the cash to purchase a new bus for $150,000. Must Big Yellow Taxi recognize gross income? What will be Big Yellow Taxi's basis in the new bus?

CHAPTER 8

TAXATION OF PERIODIC INCOME FROM CAPITAL

SECTION 2. TAX DEFERRED AND TAX-EXEMPT INVESTMENT ACCOUNTS

1. Your client is a young professional person who has $5,000 of earned income available for investment this year and is considering investing in a whole life insurance policy, a deferred annuity, tax-exempt bonds, an IRA, or a Roth IRA. Based on tax considerations, which option would you suggest?

2. Under an income tax, is exempting income from capital tantamount to adopting a system of consumption taxation?

SECTION 3. SPECIAL TREATMENT OF CORPORATE DIVIDENDS

1. Why does the House Report state that the law as it existed before enactment of the provision taxing dividends at capital gains rates "encourages corporations to finance using debt rather than equity?"

2.Do you agree that if dividends are not taxed at a preferential rate, management is discouraged from paying dividends? Might management be predisposed to not paying dividends, thus increasing the amount available for use in the business?

3. What segment of the population is most likely to benefit from the preferential rates for dividends?

SECTION 4. TAX-EXEMPT INTEREST ON STATE AND LOCAL BONDS

1. Arnold sold his farm for $10 million to the state of California, which will use the property for a state prison. The state paid Arnold $1 million in cash and gave him a promissory note for $9 million. The note pays 10 percent annual interest. May Arnold exclude the interest he earns each year from his gross income?

2. Maria was interested in buying some municipal bonds, the interest on which is exempt from tax. Although the bonds paid a lower rate of interest (6 percent) than comparable taxable bonds (which were paying 7.5 percent), Maria figured that the exemption feature would provide her a better after-tax return on the exempt bonds than on the taxable bonds. Nevertheless, she said that she was now questioning that conclusion because her investment advisor had told her that the tax-exempt bonds carried an "implicit tax."

   (a) Can you explain to Maria what the investment advisor meant?

   (b) Does the existence of such an implicit tax mean that the tax-exempt bonds are actually not a good deal for Maria, who is in the 35 percent marginal rate bracket?

3. Should § 103 be repealed? How do equity and efficiency concerns affect your argument? Is the federal income tax system the proper vehicle through which to pursue policies such as subsidizing state and local governments?

SECTION 5. TREATMENT OF THE OWNER OF ANNUITY AND LIFE INSURANCE CONTRACTS

1. Twenty years ago Hume purchased a whole life insurance policy that would pay his wife, Jessica, $2 million upon his death. The premium was $20,000 per year.

   (a) Under the terms of the policy, currently Hume could surrender the policy for its cash value of $975,000, which is $575,000 more than Hume has paid in premiums over the last 20 years. Has Hume realized any gross income over the past 20 years?

   (b) If Hume dies and the insurance company pays his widow, Jessica, the $2 million death benefit, how much gross income does she recognize?

(c) Suppose instead that Hume surrendered the policy for its $975,000 cash surrender value the day before he died. How much gross income would he have to recognize?

2. Carson decides to purchase an annuity. The lump sum premium is $30,000 and the annuity will pay Carson $3,000 annually; Carson's life expectancy is only 15 years.

(a) What are the tax implications when Carson receives his first $3,000 payment?

(b) Suppose Carson dies after year eight. His annuity provides no payments after death. What are the tax implications?

(c) Suppose Carson surpasses his life expectancy. What are the tax implications when he receives his payment in the sixteenth year?

CHAPTER 9

DAMAGE AWARDS AND SETTLEMENTS AND INSURANCE RECOVERIES

SECTION 1. DAMAGES RECEIVED ON ACCOUNT OF PROPERTY AND LOST PROFITS

1. Jake's Bicycles and Karen's Bicycles are the only bicycle shops in town. Karen sells a respected line of Yolo bicycles. Jake started rumors in the local bicycle club that Karen is replacing components on Yolo bicycles with inferior products while selling the bicycles as authentic. The rumors seriously undermined Karen's bicycle sales. Karen sued Jake for tortious unfair competition leading to the destruction of the good name of Karen's Bicycles. Karen collected $30,000 of compensatory damages and $50,000 of punitive damages from Jake's Bicycles. How much of this money is includable in Karen's gross income?

2. Ansel is interested in environmental preservation. To that end, he has purchased vast amounts of land and kept it as undeveloped as possible. Recently, Ansel purchased 200 acres of land in Ohio at a cost of $2,000,000. The heavily forested area is home to the rare wood snipe. Unfortunately, in a mix-up over property lines, a logging company cut down and sold many trees that were on Ansel's land. The loggers also destroyed the main nesting areas of the wood snipe. Ansel sued the logging company and recovered a total of $1,200,000, representing the diminution in value of the land and the conversion of the lumber. How much, if any, of this recovery is gross income to Ansel?

SECTION 2. DAMAGE AWARDS FOR PERSONAL INJURY

1. Kono, the former lead singer of the rock band WD-40, was injured when he slipped on an icy sidewalk in front of a recording studio. Kono has incurred $50,000 of medical expenses and expects to incur another $25,000 of medical expenses in the future, all as a result of injuries he sustained during the fall.

Kono' injury also prevented him from performing at a concert for which he would have been paid $15,000. Kono sued the recording studio to recover all of those amounts, as well as $100,000 for the pain and suffering he has had to endure.

(a) The case proceeds to trial and Kono is awarded the full $190,000 he sought. Is this gross income to Kono?

(b) The defense offers to settle out of court for $150,000. If the recording studio's insurance company pays that amount, are the settlement proceeds gross income to Kono?

(c)Suppose instead that Kono is paid for the concert, though he is unable to perform, because the promoter believes in keeping performers happy. Is the amount received by Kono from the concert promoter gross income to Kono?

2. Snoopy, a prominent and influential voice in hip-hop, has denounced Millie, a performing musician, both through his radio show and in an article in *Rolling Stone*, asserting that Millie steals the work of unknown musicians and claims it as her own. These accusations severely hurt Millie's popularity as an individual artist. Sales of Millie's records quickly dropped, and attendance at her concerts fell off dramatically. Alleging that she lost $700,000 in earnings and had been socially ostracized, Millie sued Snoopy for defamation. She demanded $6,000,000 in compensatory damages and $15,000,000 in punitive damages. The jury agreed with Millie in all aspects of the case, and awarded her $21,000,000. How much of the award is gross income to Millie?

3. While performing a concert, Hope, a famous country singer, was injured when a spotlight, negligently attached above the stage, came crashing down. The concert promoter, who was responsible, has offered to settle the case. The promoter puts two settlement offers on the table. Under the first, Hope would receive $400,000 now. Under the second, Hope would receive $20,000 a year for 20 years, and then $400,000 at the end of that period. Assume that if Hope chose the first option, she could invest the $400,000 in a taxable bond that would pay her $20,000 a year. Based only on federal income tax considerations, which option is better for Hope?

SECTION 3. INSURANCE RECOVERIES

1. Harry Hinke is a TV cameraman for Earthwide Sports Presentations Nightly. While Harry was covering a professional basketball game from courtside, the Cook County Toro's famous basketball star, Denny Worm, ran out of bounds, tripped over a chair, knocked Harry down, and stepped on him, severely

injuring Harry. Harry retained well known plaintiff's lawyer Willie Gingrich to sue Toros, Inc., the team owner, for negligently placing the courtside chair. After trial, a judgment for $1,000,000 was entered against Toros Inc. The Toro's insurance carrier, FewState Casualty & Indemnity Co. pays Harry the $1,000,000. Does Toros, Inc. realize gross income when FewState Casualty & Indemnity pays Harry's claim?

2. A sound engineer in Moon Records recording studio in Memphis has been injured in an accident at the studio and will be unable to work for a few months.

(a) Suppose the sound engineer receives $200 a week under Tennessee workers' compensation law. Is this gross income for the sound engineer?

(b) Suppose that while the engineer is out, Moon Records voluntarily pays him $1,000 a week in addition to the amount the engineer receives under the workers' compensation plan. Is the additional $1,000 per week gross income for the sound engineer?

3. (a) During rock concerts at the local civic center, the city often has police officers stationed throughout the parking lot to direct traffic and make sure the crowds leave in an orderly and safe manner. At a recent concert by the legendary Stoney Rollers, Officer Wallace, who is only 30 years old, was permanently disabled by a negligent driver. Unable to work again, Wallace was given a disability pension of $24,000 a year by the police department. The disability pension will continue until Wallace reaches mandatory retirement age (55), at which time it will become a regular retirement pension. Are the pension payments gross income to Wallace?

(b) Suppose instead that Wallace was actually off duty, and moonlighting for the Stoney Rollers as a part-time security guard when the injury occurred. Nevertheless, he still receives the payments described above. How does this change your answer to (a)?

CHAPTER 10

INCOME FROM THE CANCELLATION OF INDEBTEDNESS

SECTION 1. GENERAL PRINCIPLES

1. Michael signs a note to repay Tony $10,000 in two years, plus five percent interest payable annually. Michael receives $9,000 of cash from Tony when he signs the note, and he pays the interest as it is due. When the loan principal is due, however, Michael is a little short. In a deal Michael can't refuse, Tony agrees to accept $9,500 of cash as repayment of the loan. Does Michael recognize gross income from this transaction?

2. Lupe guarantees her wholly owned corporation's repayment of a $100,000 loan from the Penultimate National Bank. The corporation makes principal payments of $50,000, but then fails to repay the rest of the loan. The Bank seeks to collect the $50,000 balance from Lupe pursuant to her guarantee. Ultimately Lupe and the bank compromise, and Lupe pays the Bank $40,000 in full satisfaction of the claim. Does Lupe realize $10,000 of COD income?

SECTION 2. STATUTORY CODIFICATION OF CANCELLATION OF INDEBTEDNESS RULES

1. Bert and Ernie are twins who work in identical jobs in the Biology Department of Research University. They each earn a salary of $30,000 per year. They each have the same amount of total assets. Last year they each borrowed $10,000 for a vacation in Alaska, where they spent the entire loan proceeds. Over the course of this year, Bert used $10,000 of his wages to pay off the loan. Ernie, however, is a bit of a spendthrift. He not only failed to pay off the loan, but declared bankruptcy. Ernie's debt for the vacation was discharged. Bert wants to know why he has to pay taxes on the $10,000 that he spent on his vacation and repaid, while Ernie not only does not have to repay the $10,000, but is also relieved of any federal income taxes on the $10,000 he spent on his vacation. Can you explain to Bert why this is fair?

2. Suppose the facts are the same as in Problem 1, except that Ernie does not have to pay his $10,000 debt because he goes to his creditor, tells the creditor that he is suffering financial difficulties and cannot repay the loan, and the creditor forgives the debt. Further assume that Ernie is insolvent at that time by more than $10,000. Does your answer change? How?

3. Oscar has accumulated $15,000 of debt on his last remaining credit card. Oscar has been able to keep up with the interest payments (finance charges) but is falling behind in paying the $15,000 of principal. Oscar's total debt to his creditors, including the credit card, is $80,000. Oscar has only $70,000 of assets consisting of $12,000 of cash, 100 shares of Biochem, Inc. stock that have a fair market value of $14,000 and a basis of $9,000, and other property, including furniture, his car, jewelry, and miscellaneous personal items worth $44,000. How much gross income must Oscar recognize if the credit card company accepts $12,000 cash as full repayment of the debt?

4. Several years ago, Berkshire, Warren & Co., LLC, an investment banking firm, purchased 1,000,000 shares of Outron Corporation preferred stock directly from the corporation for $100,000,000. Berkshire paid for the stock by giving Outron a promissory note for $100,000,000, due in 20 years, with interest payable annually at 2 percent, which was then the prevailing market rate. Recently, Outron decided that it needed to increase its current cash flow and offered Berkshire a reduction of the principal amount of the promissory note to $80,000,000 if Berkshire would agree to increase the interest rate to the current market rate, which is substantially in excess of 2 percent. Berkshire found the offer advantageous and accepted it. How much COD income does Berkshire realize?

5. Several years ago, Courtney borrowed $160,000 from the Friendly Local Bank and used it to buy an apartment building. The Bank held a mortgage on the apartment building as security for the loan. Courtney has not been able to rent any of the apartments in the building and has not made any principal payments on the loan, but she has paid all of the interest due. Courtney has fallen on hard times and her only assets are $60,000 in cash and the apartment building, which is now worth $55,000 and which now has an adjusted basis of $96,000. If the Bank accepts $60,000 in cash from Courtney in full discharge of her debt, how much gross income must Courtney recognize?

SECTION 3. THE DISPUTED DEBT, OR CONTESTED LIABILITY DOCTRINE

1. Last year Hillary Homeowner hired Ralph Roofer to put a new roof on her house. When the job was complete Hillary gave Ralph a personal check for $10,000. How much income does Hillary realize if the check is not negotiated under the following circumstances?

   (a) Ralph deposited the check but it was returned for insufficient funds. Subsequently Ralph lost the check. Although Hillary wondered what happened to the check, she never followed up with Ralph. The statute of limitations on collecting the check has now run.

   (b) Shortly after the roof was completed, it rained and the roof leaked. Hillary instructed her bank not to honor the check. Hillary and Ralph subsequently agreed that Ralph would accept $6,000 in payment for the roof.

2. While skiing in Idaho, PicaBoo was severely injured when Spike, an out-of-control snowboarder, crashed into her while PicaBoo was waiting in line at the ski lift. PicaBoo secured a verdict against Spike for $100,000. Spike appealed and pending the appeal, PicaBoo accepted Spike's offer to settle for $60,000. Must Spike recognize $40,000 of cancellation of indebtedness income?

SECTION 4. CANCELLATION OF INDEBTEDNESS AS A MEDIUM OF PAYMENT

1. Five years ago Captain Jack borrowed $100,000 from the Fourth National Bank. He used the loan proceeds to purchase a boat to ferry passengers across the Mississippi River. The loan requires payments of interest only for the first six years with a balloon payment due at the end of the sixth year. Captain Jack has paid the interest when due. The ferryboat business has not been doing well. Captain Jack's assets are limited to his personal residence, in which he has $30,000 of equity, $20,000 of cash, miscellaneous personal property including a car worth $10,000, and the ferryboat which is now worth $60,000 but in which Captain Jack has an adjusted basis of $10,000 (due to depreciation deductions). The Fourth National Bank agrees to accept the boat plus $15,000 of cash as repayment of the loan in full. Does Captain Jack recognize gross income from this arrangement?

2. (a) Dawn went to work for the Fortunata Corporation right after law school. Fortunata was so happy to have recruited Dawn that it paid off her student loans. What is the tax consequence to Dawn?

(b) Instead of going to work for Fortunata Corporation, Dawn goes to work for the Internal Revenue Service and her law school's SPIN (Student Public Interest Network) program gives her $3,000 to help pay off her student loans. What are the tax consequences to Dawn?

(c) Instead of going either of the above, Dawn went to work for a public interest law firm that is an I.R.C. § 501(c)(3) charitable organization. The terms of the Dawn's student loan from the law school provided that the loan would be forgiven if Dawn worked for an I.R.C. § 501(c)(3) charitable organization for at least five years after graduation. Dawn worked at the public interest law firm for six years and the loan was forgiven. What is the tax consequence to Dawn?

3. Felicia is a talented telemarketer. She has only $70,000 of assets, but has accumulated total debts of $80,000, including $15,000 of debt on her last remaining credit card. Felicia has been able to keep up with the interest payments (finance charges) but is falling behind in paying the $15,000 of principal. How much gross income must Felicia recognize if she agrees to provide, and does provide, a two-week training session for the credit card company's telemarketing supervisors. Normally Felicia would receive $12,000 for such a training session. The credit card company agrees to cancel Felicia's $15,000 debt in exchange for the training session.

4. Ritchie's father, Howard, lent Ritchie $25,000 to help Ritchie buy an interest in Fonzi's car repair business. Several years later, when the loan was still outstanding and Ritchie got married, Howard cancelled the loan "to help out the happy couple." Does Ritchie recognize COD income?

CHAPTER 11

TAX EXPENDITURES

SECTION 1. THE CONCEPT OF TAX EXPENDITURES

1. Tax expenditures are said to be the equivalents of direct government spending programs. Yet, a taxpayer benefiting from a tax expenditure does not receive a check from the government. What hypothetical construct regarding payment of taxes and receipt of a subsidy must lie behind the assertion of equivalency?

2. After Picard and Janeway retired, they took up farming in the United States. Picard receives a check in the amount of $1,000 from the government to pay for the costs of mandated soil conservation programs. Janeway is entitled to a tax credit of $1,000 for not planting her entire farm acreage. Are Picard and Janeway treated alike for federal income tax purposes? If not, why not, and what steps would be required to treat them equally for federal income tax purposes?

3. Congress passes a law that defers the inclusion of certain income that Kirk, also long since retired, has received. What is the nature of the implicit expenditure program? Would or should the provision be objectionable on tax policy grounds if Congress imposed an interest charge on Kirk's (and others') deferred income taxes?

4. Janeway faces a marginal rate of 35 percent on her next dollar of income. Picard faces a marginal rate of 10 percent on his next dollar of income. Why would a deduction of $100 to each be worth more to Janeway than to Picard?

5. You are working on the staff of Senator Marbury, who asks you to consider the exclusions from income that result under §§ 105-106. The Senator would like you to tell him what changes would have to be made to those provisions if they are to operate like a directly funded national health insurance program.

6. Senator Marbury has noted that the realization requirement is not listed as a tax expenditure. He would like you to tell him what arguments support its inclusion in that category. Are there any arguments to the contrary?

7. Senator Marbury also wants to know whether the arguments in support of including the realization requirement as a tax expenditure also apply to including the non-taxation of imputed income as a tax expenditure.

PART III

BUSINESS DEDUCTIONS AND CREDITS

CHAPTER 12

ORDINARY AND NECESSARY BUSINESS AND PROFIT-SEEKING EXPENSES

SECTION 1. THE RELEVANCE OF "TRADE OR BUSINESS" VERSUS "PROFIT-SEEKING" EXPENSES

1. Herbert Walker is the owner of a profitable fried pork rind factory, where he works as the general manager. Herb devotes approximately 200 days per year to the pork rind business. During the rest of his time, Herb devotes himself to investing for his own account online. He is online at least once every day for a minimum of one hour, he does not employ the services of a broker, and he

makes money on the daily swings in the price of the stock he purchases. Over the last five years Herb has made over $700,000 from his investment activities. Herb incurs approximately $10,000 in expenses for supplies and other incidentals needed to manage his investments. Is Herb engaged in a trade or business or an activity for the production of income? Does it matter?

SECTION 2. THE "ORDINARY AND NECESSARY" LIMITATION

1. Noted pop singer Max Haggard opened a restaurant in Bakersfield, California, featuring real hamburgers and milkshakes (a lost taste). The business was incorporated as Anti-Donalds, Inc. Max financed the corporation mostly by corporate borrowing from Max's friends and sponsors. Unfortunately, there is little demand for real hamburgers and milkshakes, and the business ultimately failed. Max, having sold the investment to his friends, paid off the loans in full, approximately $100,000, even though he was under no legal obligation to do so. Nonetheless, Max was aware that not paying the loans could adversely affect his singing career. His annual income from his recording career exceeds $1 million. Can Max deduct the loan repayments under § 162?

2. Elle is a new associate in the large Miami law firm of Wewanna, Earn, & Bill. Elle spent a week in Santa Fe, New Mexico, reviewing a transaction on behalf of a large client. Elle spent $125 per day for her hotel room, which was reasonable. Elle wanted to impress her employer with her frugal habits and decided not to request reimbursement from the firm for her hotel bill, telling the firm that she stayed with a friend. May Elle deduct her lodging expense for the trip?

SECTION 3. THE LIMITATION OF "UNREASONABLE" COMPENSATION

1. (a) John is the president and a shareholder of GreenSteel Corp., which manufactures high-grade stainless steel designed for use in top-of-the-line kitchen appliances and uses environment-friendly techniques. GreenSteel was founded many years ago by John and his friend Andrew. John and Andrew each originally owned half the stock of the corporation. John's original employment contract provided that he would receive a salary of $100,000 per year and a bonus equal to 25 percent of profits. Andrew retired last year but kept his stock. As a result of Andrew's retirement, John had to work harder. He also decided to embark upon a marketing plan that emphasized the company's environmental focus. John caused GreenSteel to give him a new contract at a salary of $200,000 per year, with a bonus equal to 50 percent of

profits. For the last five years the business has been fairly consistent. Sales have been $2 million and profits about $300,000, annually. Prior to Andrew's retirement no dividends were paid. Since Andrew's retirement, each of John and Andrew has received dividends of $20,000 annually. In an audit, the IRS disallowed GreenSteel's compensation deduction in excess of $100,000 for last year, the first year of John's $200,000 salary and increased bonus. What arguments can you make on behalf of the corporation in support of the deduction? How should compensation in excess of $100,000 be treated if the IRS prevails?

(b) Does your assessment of John's salary change if GreenSteel is publicly traded and its share price increases at the same rate as the Dow Jones Industrial average?

2. GreenSteel also paid John's son, Clint, $25,000 to be the sales manager for the Monterey, California district. Clint, who is a junior at the University of California at Carmel, spent three or four Saturdays (a total of twenty hours for the year) visiting kitchen design stores to tout products made with GreenSteel's products and the environmental consciousness of the company. GreenSteel had gross sales in California last year of $10,000. The IRS has disallowed GreenSteel's deduction of Clint's salary in excess of $2,000. How should Clint, John, and GreenSteel treat the excess $23,000?

SECTION 4. EXPENSES RELATED TO TAX-EXEMPT INCOME

1. Marie Curie works as a physicist for Uranium, Inc., a nuclear energy research corporation. Marie received a $10,000 scholarship from the National Science Foundation to return to MIT for a nine-month course in nuclear physics and the receipt of a master's degree, in order to help advance her groundbreaking research at Uranium, Inc. After completing the course and returning to Uranium, Marie deducted the $10,000 cost of the course on her tax return, pursuant to § 162 and Treas. Reg. § 1.162-5. Is the Internal Revenue Service likely to allow the deduction?

SECTION 5. "PUBLIC POLICY" LIMITATIONS: TAX PENALTIES

1. Mark Mobile owns a chain of gas stations. Mark paid a $25,000 bribe to the distribution manager of Particulate Air Refinery, Inc., which was Mark's primary supplier, in order to assure a supply of gasoline during a time of shortages. Is Mark's payment deductible as an ordinary and necessary business expense?

2. The state legislature has adopted a ballot initiative to ban smoking in all buildings that are open to the public. Emphysema-R-Us, Inc., a major cigarette company, believes that passage of the initiative will seriously undercut the profits of its local operation. Emphysema-R-Us undertakes a statewide television campaign urging voters not to adopt the initiative and stating that the initiative will unfairly restrict the citizens' "constitutional right" to consume. Also, Emphysema-R-Us lobbies the Metropolis City Council to adopt a resolution against the initiative, pointing out the loss of sales tax revenue to the City. Are Emphysema-R-Us's expenditures in this campaign deductible?

CHAPTER 13

DEDUCTIBLE PROFIT-SEEKING EXPENSES VERSUS NONDEDUCTIBLE CAPITAL EXPENDITURES

SECTION 2. EXPENDITURES TO ACQUIRE OR PRODUCE TANGIBLE PROPERTY

1. In 2015, Alex purchased raw land. The purchase price was $150,000, but in addition to the purchase price, Alex paid a real estate broker, a $5,500 commission for assisting with finding and closing the transaction. Earlier this year, Alex sold the raw land. The selling price was $175,000, but Alex paid a real estate broker a $6,500 commission to list the property and help close the sale. May Alex deduct either of the brokerage commissions? What was his basis for the stock? What was his amount realized on the sale? Does he recognize gain or loss?

2. Moe operates a sandwich shop and bar across the street from the campus of Gator State University. Several years ago, MacAdam, who owns and operates a commercial parking lot across the street adjacent to Moe's Deli, repaved and expanded his parking lot. Recently, Moe decided to expand by adding patio seating to Moe's Deli, and he discovered that MacAdam's parking lot encroached on Moe's land. Moe incurred $20,000 of legal fees in a suit to compel MacAdam to remove the encroaching pavement. Can Moe properly deduct the attorney's fees or are they a capital expenditure?

3. Vanessa, an experienced real estate developer, purchased a rundown apartment complex from Tommy Tenement for $500,000. As Vanessa began renovation, she discovered that all of the water and sewage connections were substandard, contrary to representations that Tommy had made as part of the sales agreement. Vanessa obtained estimates that it would cost $100,000 to repair the pipes. She filed suit against Tommy for misrepresentation, claiming $100,000 of damages. The suit was settled for $80,000. Vanessa's attorney

retained $30,000 of the settlement as his fee. May Vanessa deduct the $30,000 of attorney's fees?

4. Bassamatic Corp. manufactures specialty food processors for use in preparing seafood recipes. Last year Bassamatic incurred the following expenses:

Depreciation on factory (building & equipment)

	$ 200,000
Cost of parts to manufacture Bassamatics	$1,000,000
Salaries of factory workers	$2,000,000
Electric and Utilities for factory	$ 300,000
Rent for corporate offices	$ 250,000
Salaries of president, sales personnel and administrative assistants	$ 500,000

To what extent are these expenditures deductible and to what extent must they be capitalized?

SECTION 3. AMOUNTS PAID TO IMPROVE TANGIBLE PROPERTY

1. (a) Tritium Labeling Corp. ("TLC"), installed filters that remove tritium residue from a large smoke stack on its property at a cost of $1 million. When installed five years ago, the filters had a useful life of ten years. TLC's plant cost $50 million when constructed and had an expected useful life of 25 years. Under the current administration, the EPA has lowered its standards for radioactive emissions, which would enable TLC to bypass its filters and improve the efficiency of its operations at an annual savings of $750,000. TLC spent $250,000 to install a system to bypass the filters. Is this expenditure deductible?

(b) Four years later, a new EPA administrator decided to tighten emissions regulations, and threatened to close down TLC's operation unless it reinstated its filtering operation. TLC is required to spend $500,000 to renovate and reactivate the filters. Is this amount deductible?

2. The Decker Towing Company of San Francisco Bay operates a fleet of tugboats. Each tugboat typically costs $2 million and has an expected useful life of 15 years. As part of a regular preventative maintenance program Decker overhauls each of the two diesel engines in its tugs every three years. The overall costs amount to $100,000. This year, during its second maintenance cycle, Decker replaced one of the engines in its tug Sgt. Schultz at a cost of $500,000 because the engine had been particularly troublesome, causing a lot

of down time for the tug. Is the cost of the overhauls deductible? May Decker deduct the cost of the new engine in Sgt. Schultz?

3. High Octane, Inc. has operated a service station and automobile repair business in Bakersfield for over two decades. Recently High Octane discovered that a leaky storage tank has contaminated the soil under High Octane's property. High Octane replaced the tank at a cost of $300,000; with the new tank there will be no soil contamination in the future. In addition, High Octane will incur substantial costs to clean up the soil. May High Octane deduct any of these costs?

SECTION 4. COSTS TO ACQUIRE OR CREATE INTANGIBLES

1. Usury Finance Co. is a large consumer credit lender. Last year it lent $1 billion to approximately 50,000 customers – the average loan was $20,000. Most of these loans are for a three- to seven-year term and are secured by a car, boat, or other consumer durable. To make these loans Usury Finance employs 50 loan officers who process applications. Their aggregate salaries last year totaled $1,000,000. Usury Finance also paid outside legal counsel $800,000 last year to prepare loan forms and provide other legal services in connection with making and securing the loans, as well as $500,000 in filing fees for UCC-2 statements to secure the loans. To what extent are these expenditures deductible and to what extent must they be capitalized?

2. Looking for more shop space, Keith paid $75,000 to Hector in exchange for Hector assigning his rights in a lease for shop. The assignment was effective August 1, and the lease required $4,000 monthly rental payments and had 4.5 years remaining on it. May Keith deduct the $75,000 or monthly rent payments?

3. On December 10, Year 17, Jared paid $35,000 to Beneficial Insurance Corp. for a fire insurance policy that covered his business from January 1 to December 31 of Year 18. To what extent, if any may Jared deduct the $35,000? Would the answer change, if the policy covered February 1, Year 18, to January 31, Year 19?

SECTION 5. BUSINESS INVESTIGATIONS, START-UP AND EXPANSION COSTS

1. WasteDisposal Inc., is a large waste treatment concern that operates in Nevada and surrounding states. WasteDisposal recently constructed a new waste treatment plant in Nevada. It paid $300,000 for a television advertising

campaign to convince Nevada residents of the desirability of waste treatment plants, stressing the creation of jobs. In addition, when the plant was nearing completion, WasteDisposal began a training program for plant operators. The training program ran for five months prior to initiating waste treatment at the plant. Salaries and other expenses for the training program were $400,000. To what extent are these expenditures deductible and to extent must they be capitalized?

2. Outrun Gas and Electric, Inc. is a large Texas-based power company that supplies electricity to much of the southwest and Pacific coast. All of Outrun's existing generating plants are oil-fired. Outrun needs to build a new plant to service its increasing number of customers and with the increasing price of oil, Outrun believes that a new nuclear power plant would be much more profitable than another oil-fired power plant. Outrun therefore spent $2,000,000 on a feasibility study to determine whether building a new nuclear power plant would be more profitable than building another oil-fired plant. Outrun also spent $5,000,000 on advertising designed to reduce opposition to nuclear power plants. It eventually constructed the new nuclear power plant. Are the costs of conducting the feasibility study and advertising deductible by Outrun?

3. After a successful and highly paid career as a World-cup racer, Sarah Skier decided to open a ski shop. Sarah investigated four shops that were for sale in Colorado, Northern New Mexico, and Montana. She spent $3,300 on transportation, meals, and lodging to travel to the locations of each potential business opportunity, or $800 per ski shop with respect to each of the three shops she investigated but did not purchase, and $900 with respect to the shop she purchased. Sarah spent $600 in legal and accounting fees to investigate each of the four shops. She spent $1,500 in legal and accounting fees to negotiate acquisition of the business, located in Montana, that she purchased. Pending the closing of her acquisition, Sarah made two trips to the East Coast to consult with the manufacturers of ski lines that she was planning to carry. Each of these trips cost $1,200. Following acquisition of the shop, which she renamed Sarah's Big Sky Ski Shop, she closed the shop for two weeks to reorganize the inventory, install a line of bicycles, and train employees to deal with the customers. She paid employee salaries of $2,000 during this two-week period. One week after she opened the doors to customers, Sarah traveled to Vermont to meet with representatives of a third line of ski gear. This trip cost $1,500. Which, if any, of these expenses are deductible by Sarah?

4. Jacques Fischer has been searching for the wreck of the Flying Dutchman, a 17th century shipwreck. In the past three years Jacques spent $100,000 searching, but had no luck. This year, after spending another $20,000, he found the wreck and recovered gold and silver artwork and bronze cannons

worth over $1,000,000. Thereupon he opened a for-profit museum in Key West devoted to the wreck of the Flying Dutchman, where he displayed the artifacts and earned a handsome living from admission fees. To what extent are these expenditures deductible and to what extent must they be capitalized?

5. Outrun Gas and Electric, Inc. is a large Texas-based power company that supplies electricity to much of the southwest and Pacific coast. Due to recent power shortages in some of the states served by Outrun that have deregulated electricity prices, Outrun believes that it can increase profits by constructing additional generating facilities. To this end, Outrun spent $250,000 on a feasibility study examining whether potential expansion and construction of an additional nuclear power plant would be a profitable endeavor. Outrun then incurred $200,000 for engineering, accounting, and legal fees to obtain approval from the Texas Public Utility Commission to construct the new plant. After receiving the required approvals Outrun incurred the following expenditures: (1) land acquisition, $750,000; (2) legal fees for land acquisition, $40,000; (3) title insurance, $20,000; (4) engineering and legal fees to obtain a Nuclear Regulatory Commission permit, $300,000; (5) legal fees to negotiate construction contract, $100,000; (6) plant construction, $150,000,000. In addition, two of Outrun's regularly employed engineers, whose aggregate salaries totaled $800,000, supervised construction of the plant over several years. To what extent are these expenditures deductible and to what extent are they capital expenditures?

CHAPTER 14

COST RECOVERY MECHANISMS

SECTION 1. DEPRECIATION

A. ACCELERATED COST RECOVERY SYSTEM

B. ELECTION TO EXPENSE CERTAIN DEPRECIABLE BUSINESS ASSETS

1.(a) Lisa runs a company that takes radioactive waste from the local nuclear power plant and converts it into protein drinks (what they lack in taste, they make up for in environmental friendliness). In January 2016, she purchases a building and the latest in computer technology for the company. Lisa also buys several expensive photographs depicting Lake Springfield's appearance before it was ruined by pollution, to hang in her office. Finally, as a reward to herself for her hard work, Lisa purchases a pony, for recreational use with her sister on the weekends. What items may Lisa depreciate?

(b) Assume the building may be depreciated. Lisa purchased the building and the land upon which it sits for $1,200,000 in cash, of which $1,000,000 was attributable to the building and $200,000 was attributable to the land. However, shortly after her acquisition, the Springfield real estate market took off and the land and building are now valued at $2,000,000. How does this affect the depreciation deductions allowable with respect to the building?

(c) Many years into the future, long after Lisa has depreciated the full amount of the building, the land and building are valued at $4,000,000. If Lisa decides to sell, what will be her taxable gain?

2. (a) Lisa also purchases machinery to mass-produce her "ProtonPower" protein drinks, which she places in service after January 1. The machinery costs $1,400,000 and has a twelve-year class-life in Lisa's business. At that time, the resale value of the machinery is estimated to be $450,000. What depreciation deductions may she take each year?

(b) What are the tax consequences if Lisa sells the equipment for $450,000 at the end of year three? What if she sells it instead for $350,000?

3. (a) On February 1 of this year Mona bought a small apartment building for $2 million ($400,000 representing the value of the land). She immediately begins to rent apartments to local college students. What are Mona's depreciation deductions for the first ten years?

(b) Mona paid Leonardo $40,000 to plant trees around the building and generally improve the landscaping. Can she depreciate this capitalized expense?

(c) Mona leased an undeveloped plot of land for 35 years. She constructs a small building and begins operating a bed and breakfast. Can Mona depreciate the cost of the building? Over what period? Would your answer change if Mona leased the land for 20 years?

4. Leonardo operated a landscaping business. He purchased a backhoe at the start of July for $80,000. For the next month and a half, Leonardo used the backhoe to assist in remodeling the building where he stores his landscaping equipment. From August 15 until November 15, Leonardo used the backhoe to perform work for various customers of his business. On November 16, Leonardo suspended operation of the landscaping business indefinitely and started working as a house painter. The backhoe was used occasionally during the next month and a half only to construct a koi pond in Leonardo's back yard. Leonardo did not elect to expense the backhoe under I.R.C § 179. What depreciation deductions may Leonardo claim? Assume the backhoe has a five-year cost recovery period.

5. Glowing Waters Electric Power Corp., acquired additional nuclear reactor fuel assemblies that comprised a new "reactor core." During December, Year 1, and January Year 2, the assemblies were inspected, installed, and tested. In February, Year 2,, the reactor in which they were installed, which had been idle since mid-December of the prior year, was restarted. Is Glowing Waters entitled to begin depreciating the cost of the new nuclear reactor fuel assemblies in Year 1 or must it wait until Year 2?

SECTION 2. STATUTORY AMORTIZATION OF INTANGIBLE ASSETS

1. Caffeine-Cola, Inc. the world's largest soft-drink bottler, purchased Lisa's ProtonPower protein drinks company (which was unincorporated). In addition to the land, buildings, and machinery, the deal included, among other things, the secret formula for ProtonPower protein drinks (valued at $1,500,000), a patent Lisa owns for an innovative new bottling technique ($600,000), Lisa's customer list ($450,000), and an easement over her neighbor's land that provides easy access to the highway ($60,000).

(a) How can Caffeine-Cola recover the cost of the formula for ProtonPower, the customer list, the easement, and the patent?

(b) Suppose instead that Caffeine-Cola buys only Lisa's bottling patent, which has six years remaining. Does this change your answer to (a) with respect to the patent?

SECTION 3. EXPENSING AND AMORTIZATION PROVISIONS

1. Tucker, a young mechanical engineer, inherited millions of dollars when his parents recently died. He quit his job designing automotive power train parts for Toyota-Ford, USA Inc. to devote his energies to developing an automobile engine that runs on carbonated water. So far he has spent $850,000 in his attempt, and although he has made some progress, he has not yet developed a successful water powered automobile engine. May Tucker either deduct or amortize his $850,000 of expenditures?

SECTION 4. CAPITAL RECOVERY FOR NATURAL RESOURCES

1. Slim Pickins, an oil tycoon, purchased an operating oil well from ShellExxonMobilBP. The well cost $5.5 million, of which $5 million is attributable to the oil reserves in the ground and $500,000 is attributable to machinery and equipment (pumps, pipes, tanks, etc.). Slim's analysts expect the well to produce a total of 2 million barrels of oil. In the first year, the well produces 30,000 barrels, which Slim sells for an average of $40 a barrel, excluding any refining or transportation costs. How may Slim recover the cost of the well?

2. The percentage depletion method allows the taxpayer to continue to take deductions even after the basis is reduced to zero. What do you suppose is the rationale behind this rule?

3. Hunter Bunk, a Texas oil tycoon, spent $3,000,000 (in addition to the cost of equipment) to drill an oil well. The well was a gusher and is expected to produce significant quantities of oil for the next ten years. How does Hunter recover the $3,000,000 cost of drilling the oil well?

CHAPTER 15

TRANSACTIONAL LOSSES

SECTION 1. BUSINESS OR PROFIT SEEKING LOSSES

1. Donald, a real estate developer, sold three houses that he owned. One was his personal residence that sold for $250,000, and in which Donald had a basis of $400,000. The second was Donald's Panama City vacation home that cost him $150,000, which he sold for $275,000. The third was a rental unit located in Weed, California that Donald has rented consistently for years, in which he had an adjusted basis of $175,000 and which sold for $100,000. How do Donald's gains and losses affect his taxable income?

2. Ted had a vacation home on Cape Cod. His basis in this home was $300,000. On January 1 three years ago Ted was offered $275,000 for the home. Ted accepted the offer, but the purchaser backed out on discovering that the beach was eroding in front of the house. Ted then rented the house on February 1, and continued to rent it for the next two years. Ted properly claimed $10,000 of depreciation deductions in each of the two years. Last year, Ted sold the property for $250,000. How much, if anything, is Ted able to deduct as a result of the sale of the house?

3. Dana Diver purchased a dive boat for $200,000. (She did not claim nor was she entitled to any expense deduction under § 179.) Dana used the boat in her charter and dive boat business 60 percent of the time. She used the boat for personal diving trips for herself and her friends the remaining 40 percent of the time. While she owned the boat, Dana properly claimed $80,000 of depreciation deductions, based on her 60 percent business use. Dana sold the boat for $90,000. What is Dana's deductible loss and/or includable gain on the sale of the boat?

4. (a) Anthony purchased a shopping center building for $3,000,000, paying $1,000,000 for the land and $2,000,000 for the building. Four years later, when the basis for the building was $1,750,000, the shopping center burned to the ground. At the time the fair market value of the land was $2,000,000 and the fair market value of the building was $1,200,000. Does Anthony have a deductible loss, and if so, how much?

(b) What if Anthony received an insurance recovery of $1,000,000?

(c) The insurance company suspected arson and undertook an investigation. In the year following the fire, Anthony settled the claim with the insurance company and received $750,000. Does Anthony have a deductible loss, in which year, and how much?

(d) What if Anthony never filed an insurance claim but the maximum recovery under his insurance policy was $1.4 million?

5. (a) Jon M.S. Ville purchased a city block in the center of downtown Gainesville. The purchase price included $2 million for land and $500,000 for buildings. Jon continued to rent the buildings to existing tenants for two years while he developed plans for the construction of a twenty story office tower that will cost $19 million to build. Jon demolished the buildings when their adjusted bases totaled $475,000. The demolition cost Jon $100,000. Does Jon have a deductible loss for the demolition of the old buildings? What is Jon's basis in the new tower?

(b) Would your answer change if after owning the property for five years Jon discovered that the asbestos insulation had become friable and was ordered to remediate the environmental hazard; after considering that remediation would cost $1 million but that demolition would cost only $100,000, Jon demolished the buildings?

SECTION 2. LOSS DISALLOWANCE RULES

1. (a) Martha sold 100 shares of Inside Redecorating Corp. stock to her daughter Buffy, for $6,000. Martha had purchased the stock two years ago for $8,000. Eighteen months later, Buffy sold the Inside Redecorating stock for $7,000. Do Martha and Buffy recognize gain or loss on these sales?

(b) What if Buffy sold the stock for $9,000?

(c) What if Buffy sold the stock for $5,000?

2. (a) Frasier purchased 200 shares of Moonbucks Corp. common stock for $10,000 on January 1. He sold the stock on November 30 for $8,000. On December 30, Frasier purchased 200 shares of Moonbucks common stock for $8,500. Does Frasier recognize a loss? What is his basis in the Moonbucks shares?

(b) Does your answer change if Frasier made his second purchase on December 31?

3. (a) Alex, a land speculator, purchased a tract of undeveloped land several years ago for $20,000. This year, when its value was $15,000, Alex sold the land to Acres Corp. for $15,000. Alex's wife, Beth, owns 50 percent of the stock of Acres Corp., and his wife's sister, Claire, owns 50 percent. May Alex deduct his loss?

(b) What would your answer be if Alex's two brothers owned Acres Corp. in equal shares?

Section 3. Bad Debts

1. Cameron's only profit-seeking activity is managing her extensive investment portfolio. Last year she lent $100,000 to Donny, an entrepreneur, to finance Charlie's development of a water purifier. Donny's note called for repayment at the end of two years with a six percent interest rate. The note also provided that Cameron could convert the note into a 25 percent interest in any patentable products developed by Donny. Donny's project failed, and within the year Donny filed for bankruptcy. Is Cameron entitled to claim a deduction for the bad debt? What is the character of any potential deduction?

2. Raquel lent $25,000 to her son Pablo, who agreed to repay the loan in two years with interest of six percent. Pablo did not sign a promissory note, nor was the debt secured. Pablo made one annual interest payment, but then stopped making payments. Pablo now has no assets. May Raquel claim a deduction for the unpaid balance of the debt?

3. Last year, Dylan, a cash-method taxpayer, performed the legal work to form the Haight-Ashbury Neighborhood Radio Corporation. Dylan billed the corporation $10,000 for his services, which included $1,000 that Dylan expended for a corporate record book and seal. This year the Haight-Ashbury Neighborhood Radio Corp. went out of business, and the corporation became inactive. The corporation paid only $1,500 of Dylan's bill. How much may Dylan deduct as a bad debt?

CHAPTER 16

INTEREST AS A PROFIT-SEEKING EXPENSE

SECTION 1. WHAT IS INTEREST?

1. Voltaire purchased a building for his used CD store for $150,000. He obtained $100,000 of the purchase price with a mortgage loan from the Third National Bank. In addition to interest, Voltaire paid the bank the following amounts at the closing:

Loan Application Fee	$ 150
Credit Report Fee	$ 75
Lawyers Fees	$ 500
Loan Closing Fee (2% of Principal)	$2,000

   Are any of these amounts deductible as interest?

2. Ben Aglia recently signed a contract to purchase a hotel in Hawaii. The purchase price is $50,000,000 and the contract calls for a closing on July 1 of next year. The contract provides that Ben may delay the closing for up to six months, but every day the closing is deferred, Ben must pay the seller an additional $7,000. If Ben delays the closing for 30 days, may he deduct as interest the additional $210,000 he must pay at closing?

SECTION 3. LIMITATIONS ON THE INTEREST DEDUCTION

1. Simone owned an apartment building that she rented to tenants. The apartment building had a fair market value of $500,000. Simone borrowed $70,000, secured by a mortgage on the apartment, and used the proceeds to purchase a luxury SUV for personal use. May Simone deduct the interest on the loan?

2. Jean Paul borrowed $200,000 from Usury Bank and Trust as an unsecured personal loan and he deposited $200,000 in his personal bank account, which contained $150,000 of his other money. The following Monday he purchased a boat, which he intended to use for recreation, for $150,000. On Wednesday he

purchased equipment for his car repair business for $150,000. By the end of the year, he had paid $15,000 in interest on the Usury Bank loan. How much is deductible?

3. Last year André borrowed $500,000 from the Fifth National Bank and paid $25,000 of interest on the loan. How much of André's interest is deductible under the following circumstances:

(a) André used the proceeds to purchase fixtures and equipment for use in his book shop business.

(b) André used the proceeds to purchase a Hummer to drive his kids to school across the "rough terrain" of Brentwood, CA.

(c) André used the proceeds to purchase undeveloped land to hold as an investment. André's income included $50,000 of profit from his book shop business, $5,000 of dividend income and $10,000 of interest from certificates of deposit.

4. Nietzsche borrowed $100,000 and used the borrowed money to buy $70,000 of common stock in Growth Corp. and $30,000 of general reserve bonds issued by the State of Florida. During the year, Nietzsche paid $10,000 of interest on the loan. He received $2,000 of dividends on the Growth Corp. stock, $1,500 of interest on the State of Florida bonds, $100 interest on a money market checking account, and sold 100 shares of Agony Airlines stock for a $6,500 gain. Nietzsche has no other investments and owes no other debts. To what extent, if at all, may Nietzsche deduct the $10,000 interest paid on the loan?

5. The Metaphysical Construction Company, Inc. built an office condominium building with the intent of selling office units. Metaphysical spent $5,000,000 building the project. The construction was financed with a $4,000,000 construction loan and $1,000,000 out of Metaphysical's cash reserves. During the construction period consisting of all of last year, Metaphysical paid $240,000 of interest on the construction loan. During last year Metaphysical also owned an undeveloped parcel of land that was the site of a future project. This land was subject to a $600,000 mortgage on which Metaphysical paid $36,000 of interest for the year. How much of Metaphysical's interest expense must be capitalized into the cost of the office project?

6. Lizzie Borden purchased a $100,000 whole life insurance policy on her father's life. The policy required that Lizzie pay a premium of $5,000 annually for 15 years before the policy was paid up. Last year Lizzie borrowed the $5,000 to pay the premium. Does § 264 disallow the interest deduction?

CHAPTER 17

BUSINESS TAX CREDITS

1. What factors lead the tax writing committees of Congress to adopt tax credits instead of (a) tax deductions, (b) exemptions, or (c) direct expenditures, for the various purposes for which the general business credit is provided?

2. Assume you are a legislative assistant to Senator Monroe, a member of the Senate Finance Committee. The Work Opportunity Credit is up for extension. What questions should Senator Monroe ask in order to determine whether to vote in favor of the extension?

3. You are tax counsel for Biochem, Inc., a startup company. Biochem plans to spend $5 million on research and experimentation over the next three years. In order to maximize the tax credit under § 41, in what year(s) would you recommend that the research and experimentation costs be incurred?

4. Review the Joint Committee staff analysis of the low income housing credit in paragraph 4.2 of the *Detailed Analysis* in the text. Would its analysis change if Congress provided direct subsidies for low income housing which were identical in amount to the tax credit?

PART IV

Dual Purpose Expenses

Chapter 18

Determining When a Taxpayer is Engaging in a Business or Profit-Seeking Activity

SECTION 1. IS THERE A PROFIT-SEEKING MOTIVE?

1. Charles is a wealthy investment banker, who likes to play polo with his friends on the weekends. The tournaments that Charles enters with his team always offer cash prizes, so he takes the position that he is engaged in a profit-seeking venture and deducts all of his expenses (caring for and transporting his string of polo ponies, his polo clubs, etc.). Last year, Charles earned $500 in prizes from polo tournaments. In addition, he earned $300,000 from his investment banking activities. His polo expenses for the year totaled $25,000. If the

Internal Revenue Service determines that playing polo was not a profit-seeking activity for Charles, what, if anything, is Charles entitled to deduct?

2. Dr. Kildare, who has a thriving dermatology practice, decides to open a sculpture studio on the side. Kildare promptly purchases a sculpture studio in Chelsea in New York City for cash. He also takes out a loan from the bank to pay for supplies. This year, Kildare spends $3,000 in property taxes for his studio, $1,000 in interest on the bank loan, and $10,000 on supplies and marketing for his sculpting activity. In addition, he sells $5,000 worth of sculptures (mostly to sympathetic relatives). Depending on whether or not Kildare' sculpting is determined to be for profit this year, what deductions, if any, is Kildare entitled to claim?

3. Would taxpayers with hobby losses pay more or less tax if I.R.C. § 183 were repealed?

4. Suppose that the taxpayers in Peacock v. Commissioner had, against all odds, happened to catch a fish so large that the prize money from that one catch was greater than their total loss over five straight years, even though the other four years in the sequence ended in net losses. In other words, assume that the Peacocks had only 1 profitable year out of 5, but that overall, they generated a profit when all 5 years were aggregated. Have the Peacocks satisfied the presumption of § 183(d)?

5. James is a professor of veterinary medicine at New York Ag Tech University. James earns a salary of $120,000 per year. Six years ago, James purchased a 40-acre farm, costing $200,000, to raise cattle about 10 miles from his home in Yorkshire, NY. Based on his market research, James believes that there is a special market for "range fed cattle." James spends two or three evenings a week, and most of his weekends, on the farm. James breeds his cows using champion bulls, and raises the calves for sale. It's a tough market and he has lost more money than he has made from the farm, although he has had a few profitable years. Every year he anticipates that profits will be better than the prior year. Four years ago, he turned down an offer from a qualified buyer to purchase the farm for $250,000. He keeps the farm in part because he believes that working with the cattle is good for his two children.

The net earnings history of the farm over the last six years is as follows:

Last year($5,000)
2 year ago($1,000)
3 years ago $2,000
4 years ago($ 500)
5 years ago $1,500
6 years ago($8,000)

You are preparing James's return for last year. In your opinion, are the expenses that comprised James's $5,000 loss last year from raising cattle deductible?

SECTION 2. BUSINESS USE OF RESIDENCE

1. Jesse is an assistant professor of history at NapaSonoma University. Jesse is writing a book on the influence of science and technology on wine making, which he expects will be sufficient to earn tenure. In addition, he expects the book to be profitable and has already received a $1,500 advance from the NapaSonoma University Press and a contract that provides for royalties of 20 percent of sales. Jesse requires a quiet place away from students, colleagues, and the telephone, to concentrate on the book. He has, therefore, set up one room of his three-room apartment as an office where he works exclusively on the book. May Jesse deduct a portion of his apartment rental for the home office?

2. Tyra lives in a Manhattan penthouse. Last year, she inherited a mansion on Long Island from her parents, but was too busy to spend even a single night there. She did, however, manage to rent it at fair market value to an aspiring model for 60 days during the year. How does § 280A apply to limit Tyra's deductions for expenses relating to the Long Island house?

3. Scarlett owns and lives in a nice, but not opulent, house in a suburb of Atlanta. Under normal circumstances, the house would rent for about $1,000 a month. During the Olympics, however, she was able to rent it out for $2,000/week for two weeks. What are the income tax consequences of that rental to Scarlett?

4. In addition to her house in Atlanta, Scarlett purchased a condominium unit on Amelia Island for $540,000 last July 1 to keep up her golf game. She stayed at the condominium from July 1 to July 20 for a vacation. From July 21 to September 30, she rented the condominium at fair market value, though from July 21 to July 31, the tenant was Scarlett's sister Suellen, who rented the condominium at fair market value. From November 1 to November 30, Scarlett let a book editor that she knows use the condominium without

charging any rent. Scarlett hoped to encourage the book editor to accept for publication Scarlett's memoirs, *Away on the Breeze*. During October and December, the condominium was vacant. Scarlett received a total of $24,000 for renting the condominium. She incurred the following out-of-pocket expenses: (1) realtor's commissions, $8,000; (2) mortgage interest, $12,000; (3) real estate taxes, $6,000; and (4) insurance and maintenance, $1,000. The MACRS deductions for July through December would have been $20,000 if the condominium had been used solely for business. Scarlett has asked you how the items relating to the condominium should be reported on her income tax return. What do you tell her?

CHAPTER 19

EXPENSES INVOLVING BOTH PERSONAL AND BUSINESS PURPOSES

SECTION 1. GENERAL PRINCIPLES

1. Serena, a recent graduate of Legendary Law School, began work as a litigation associate at Fish & Cage, a Boston law firm. Last year Serena spent $3,000 on three-times-a-week lunches at various restaurants near the office with a group of other associates. During these lunches they discussed recent developments, court rules, and legislation impacting their practice. To what extent may Serena deduct these expenses?

SECTION 2. TRAVEL AND RELATED EXPENSES

1. Fran lives in a lower-middle-class neighborhood in the Bronx. It costs her $3 for subway and bus fare every day to commute to her job. She works at the Plaza Hotel in Manhattan, where she is paid minimum wage to clean the hotel guests' rooms. May Fran deduct the subway and bus fare?

2. (a) Lee is an attorney living in Cleveland. He is a sole practitioner who maintains an office about three miles from his home. Lee spends about half of his time in the office. The rest of his time is spent making court appearances or taking depositions. May Lee deduct the cost of driving his car from his office to the courthouse, including parking fees?

(b) On some occasions Lee drives from his home directly to the courthouse. Is this travel deductible?

(c) Occasionally Lee drives from his home to the airport to travel to Chicago where he is trying a case. Is the travel to the airport, including parking, deductible?

(d) When Lee stays overnight in Chicago, may he deduct the cost of breakfast, lunch, and dinner? Would your answer change if you knew that when home

Lee usually has only a cup of coffee for breakfast, but when traveling, he indulges in the ubiquitous, and never inexpensive, "breakfast buffet?"

(e) When Lee travels to Chicago for the day and returns the same evening, may he deduct the cost of his lunch and dinner in Chicago?

3. (a) Eugene decides to take a year off from his full time law practice in Boston and accepts a position as a visiting professor of Trial Skills for the academic year at Santa Fe Law School. Eugene rented his Boston house for the year to a group of law students. He rented a house in Santa Fe for himself, his wife, and their two children. To what extent may Eugene deduct his Santa Fe expenses, including rent, groceries, restaurant meals, and travel between Santa Fe and Boston?

(b) After teaching at Santa Fe, Eugene was appointed by the President of the United States, who was in the first year of his first term, to serve as Chief Counsel of the Department of Homeland Security. Eugene's family returned to Boston and Eugene rented an apartment in Washington, D.C. Eugene traveled to Boston each weekend to visit his family and consult with his financial advisor about the blind trust that he created. May Eugene deduct his rent and meals in Washington and his travel between Washington and Boston?

4. During the winter from November to April, Marion works as a track coach and instructor in Los Angeles. From May through October, she works as a track coach in Chapel Hill. May Marion deduct her living expenses in either Los Angeles or Chapel Hill? Which location? What factors will determine the result?

5. Harvey Halyard is a professional sailor who constantly travels from venue to venue where he is paid handsomely to serve as crew on and maintain the world's top racing sailboats. Harvey maintains no permanent residence, generally living out of his waterproof duffel bag. Harvey stays in motels and eats at restaurants and yacht clubs. May Harvey deduct his food and lodging expenses under § 162?

6. Vera Sachs, a designer for Trendy Clothing, Inc., was recently transferred from the company's main office in New York to its new office in Miami. As was its usual practice, Trendy Clothing paid for many of the expenses associated with the move, including the following: $10,000 for Vera, her husband and three children to fly to Miami and stay in a hotel on South Beach for one week three different times to look for a house; $3,000 airfare for Vera and her family to fly to Miami when they moved; $20,000 to move their furniture and other personal effects; $6,000 for food and lodging while Vera and her family were in Miami pending closing on the new house; and $30,000 in cash as

compensation for the disruption caused by moving. How will the payment of these amounts by Trendy Clothing affect Vera's federal income tax liability for the year?

SECTION 3. BUSINESS MEALS AND ENTERTAINMENT

1. Barney Smith is a financial planner who sells a variety of investment products including mutual funds, life insurance, and annuities. Every day he eats lunch at a restaurant with a client, a prospective client, lawyers, accountants, or representatives of the companies whose products he sells. Barney pays for the lunches. Barney dines with lawyers and accountants in order to build up goodwill with people who may refer prospective clients to him. Are the costs of these meals deductible?

2. The partners of the law firm of Sea, Gull & Otter all belong to the Monterey Beach and Tennis Club. The partners hold a weekly partnership meeting at the club every Wednesday during which they discuss the firm's business for the week and the progress of their twenty associates. The partners also meet with clients and play tennis with clients at the Club. The partners' spouses and children also use the club facilities for swimming, tennis, and luncheons. To what extent may the partners deduct the cost of their lunches? To what extent may the partners deduct the club dues?

3. (a) Edith Hutton is a financial planner who sells a variety of investment products including mutual funds, life insurance, and annuities. Edith bought two tickets to the Women's World Cup Soccer finals for $60 each. She used the tickets to attend the game with Mia Bigbucks, a soccer fan, hoping that Mia would retain her to manage Mia's $1 million investment portfolio. Under which of the following circumstances may Edith deduct the cost of the tickets?

    (i) Edith and Mia did not discuss business before, during, or after the game.

    (ii) Edith and Mia discussed investment strategies during half time.

    (iii) Edith and Mia discussed investment strategies on the way to and from the game.

    (iv) Edith and Mia met in Edith's office before the game to discuss investment strategies.

    (b) If Edith purchases only a single ticket and gives the ticket to Mia, who attends the game alone, may Edith deduct the cost of the ticket?

(c) Does Mia realize gross income in any of these circumstances?

4. Wolfgang's restaurant had expenses of $800,000 in connection with meals served to customers last year. Is deduction of these expenses subject to the 50 percent limit of § 274(n)?

5. (a) Danielle Webster, a well-known attorney, attended the American Bar Association annual meeting in Honolulu, Hawaii. Danielle left her home in Hanover, N.H. early Saturday morning and arrived in Honolulu late Saturday night. Danielle spent Sunday and Monday seeing the sights and shopping. The annual meeting began on Tuesday, and Danielle dutifully attended meetings for six days, through Sunday. On Monday Danielle flew to Maui where she stayed at a resort through Wednesday. Danielle flew back to Hanover Wednesday night. To what extent are Danielle's travel expenses deductible?

(b) What if the annual meeting was held in London and Danielle traveled for the same period of time and attended the same meetings but went to Paris after the meetings, rather than to Maui?

6. (a) Michael incurred $200 of expenses for meals while on a business trip for his employer. On his return from the trip, Michael submitted meal receipts and obtained a reimbursement from his employer for the $200. What are the tax consequences of these items to Michael and the employer?

(b) What if, instead of making Michael wait for reimbursement until he returned from his trip, his employer advanced him a per diem amount of $40 for his meals for each of the five days of his business trip?

SECTION 4. STATUTORY LIMITATIONS ON DEDUCTIONS FOR CERTAIN PROPERTY

1. Bernice Baithandler is a preeminent sport-fishing guide on Monterey Bay. This year Bernice purchased a $450,000 Sportsfisher boat and a $100,000 Hummer, which is large enough to tow the boat to Mexico and other places for sports fishing competitions. Bernice uses the boat and the Hummer 40 percent of the time to take clients to sports fishing tournaments. Bernice divides the remaining 60 percent of the time between fishing on her own account in tournaments that pay cash prizes (about 25 percent of the time), and using the boat and Hummer for pleasure fishing with her buddies (the remaining 35 percent of the time). To what extent is Bernice allowed depreciation deductions for the boat and Hummer under § 280F?

SECTION 5. CLOTHING

1. (a) Steffi works as a tennis pro at the Denver Country Club. She wishes to deduct the cost of her tennis shoes, socks, and tennis outfits. What would you advise her?

    (b) What if Steffi is required to embroider the club's logo prominently on her outfits?

2. (a) Buddy works part-time as a gas station attendant in order to earn extra cash while attending the University of Texas. As part of his job, Buddy was required to purchase and wear a mechanic's uniform on which the name of the gas station is embroidered. Because "gas station chic" has been taking the South by storm this season, Buddy often wears his uniform to fraternity parties at the University of Texas. Can he deduct the cost of his uniform?

    (b) If Buddy's employer gave him the uniform for free when Buddy started to work, must Buddy recognize income?

SECTION 6. CHILD AND DEPENDENT CARE

1. Would it be more theoretically correct to provide a deduction for childcare expenses in lieu of the dependent care credit of § 21?

CHAPTER 20

EXPENDITURES INVOLVING BOTH PERSONAL AND CAPITAL ASPECTS

SECTION 1. LEGAL EXPENSES

1. Tom and Nicole were involved in a disputed no-fault divorce proceeding in which they fought over the division of property. Tom demanded a $300,000 lump sum property settlement from Nicole. Nicole objected because it would require her to sell some of the acres of her highly profitable free-range rabbit farm, thereby diminishing the business. Eventually Tom and Nicole settled for annual payments to Tom of $60,000 per year for ten years (the difference in amount being attributable to the deferred nature of the payments). Nicole incurred $50,000 of attorney's fees in negotiating this arrangement. Tom incurred $30,000 of attorney's fees. Are any of the attorney's fees deductible by Nicole or Tom? Does your answer depend on whether the annual payments he will receive from Nicole are gross income to Tom?

2. Mack Adams owns and operates a parking lot across the street from Gator State University. Moe's Deli, an adjacent business, recently constructed a patio that encroached on Mack's parking lot. Mack sued Moe for trespass, seeking damages of $10,000 for lost revenue and an injunction ordering the removal of the offending patio. Mack prevailed in his action and paid his lawyer $12,000. To what extent is the $12,000 attorney's fee deductible and to what extent must it be capitalized?

SECTION 2. EXPENSES FOR EDUCATION AND SEEKING EMPLOYMENT

1. Amanda, Barbara, and Charles all graduated from South Central State Technical University with bachelor's degrees in computer science. In which of the following cases may they deduct the cost of their further education?

(a) After graduation Amanda went to work for Lost Data Laboratories ("LDL") for two years designing computer models for high explosive events.

After two years Amanda returned to South Central State Tech to get a master's degree in computer science with an emphasis on computer simulation. After completing the degree, Amanda returned to her job at LDL at a higher salary.

(b) Barbara remained at South Central State Tech to complete her master's degree in computer science. She then went to work for the National Weather Service designing computer simulations for hurricanes.

(c) Charles went to work for LDL with Amanda modeling high explosives. After two years Charles returned to South Central State Tech to get a masters degree in applied mathematics. After completing the degree, Charles went to work for the Rural Life Insurance Company as an actuary.

2. Your client, Dr. Lewis, is a primary care physician who graduated from medical school four years ago. Dr. Lewis has explained to you that her medical education cost her $120,000 in tuition and books. She has deducted $3,000 per year with the intention of amortizing the cost of her medical education over her expected working life. She has been challenged by an Internal Revenue Service agent, who claims that the expense is not deductible because it is a personal expense. Dr. Lewis has asked your advice regarding why the Internal Revenue Service considers the cost of her medical education can be considered a nondeductible personal expense. What do you tell her?

3. During her third year of law school, after her summer clerkship with a major Megalopolis law firm, Lindsey Lawstudent was flown to New York on three separate occasions for interviews by three different firms. On each trip the firms picked up her travel expenses of $1,000. Lindsey's friend Mary Jane worked with Lindsey in the Megalopolis law firm during the summer, but Mary Jane decided that she wanted to represent indigent clients at a community legal services organization in Northern California. Mary Jane incurred travel expenses of $3,000 to travel to Northern California to talk to various community legal services organizations, none of which were able to reimburse Mary Jane's travel costs. Lindsey took a job in 400-lawyer firm in New York, and Mary Jane found a job in Ukiah, California, representing farm workers. What are the federal income tax consequences of Lindsey's and Mary Jane's travel costs?

4. After spending three years as an associate with a New York firm, Shannon decided that she wanted to become a law professor. Shannon incurred $1,500 of travel expenses to attend the American Association of Law Schools job fair, where she interviewed with several law schools. Shannon ultimately found a position with the Coastal University School of Law. May Shannon deduct her travel expenses?

PART V

Deductions And Credits for Personal Living Expenses

CHAPTER 21

Itemized Personal Deductions

Section 2. Medical Expenses

1. Kate and Lisa are identical twin sisters who both suffer from anorexia nervosa, an eating disorder; they are also heavy smokers.

(a) After spending some time in an in-patient treatment facility that specialized in eating disorders Kate and Lisa were released but ordered to attend daily sessions at the facility and to buy and consume a special high calorie nutritional supplement. Are the amounts Kate and Lisa spent on the sessions and nutritional supplements deductible (subject to the applicable percentage limits)?

(b) Kate and Lisa also joined a Smoke Enders Group. As part of the Smoke Enders program participants received group counseling and support as well as nicotine gum and patches at no extra cost. Is the cost of the Smoke Enders program deductible, subject to applicable percentage limitations?

(c) In addition to participating in Smoke Enders, Kate went to an acupuncturist who promised that in one treatment she would be free of all cravings for cigarettes. Lisa went to a hypnotist who made a similar promise. Are the costs of the acupuncturist and hypnotist deductible, subject to applicable percentage limitations?

2. Scully and Mulder work for different employers. Scully receives a salary of $100,000 per year and Mulder receives a salary of $105,000 per year. Scully's employer pays $5,000 per year for health insurance coverage for Scully, but Mulder must purchase her own health insurance. If Scully and Mulder have AGI of $100,000 and $105,000, respectively, and each incurs $20,000 of medical expenses within the meaning of § 213, only $9,000 of which are covered by insurance, how much of the expenses can each deduct?

3. On the recommendation of her physician, Mariah installed a sauna in her home. The physician felt that use of the sauna several times a day would help to alleviate Mariah's worsening asthma. The sauna cost $25,000 to install but increased the value of the house by only $5,000. How much, if any, of the cost is deductible, subject to applicable percentage limitations?

4. (a) Bruce has become increasingly concerned about his thinning hair and has gone to a hair replacement clinic for a hair transplant. If the benefit of the transplant is to make Bruce look better, is the cost deductible as a medical expense subject to applicable percentage limitations?

(b) Does your answer change if Bruce got the hair transplant on the advice of his psychotherapist who believed that enhanced self-esteem would help to improve Bruce's depression?

(c) Does your answer change if Bruce is a construction worker who is exposed to the sun for long periods of time and his dermatologist feels that hair on his head will reduce the chance of sunburn and skin cancer?

SECTION 3. CHARITABLE CONTRIBUTIONS

1. The First Church of Williamsburg has a policy whereby parishioners who make annual contributions of $1,000 or more are entitled to occupy specific pews, which also bear their names. The oldest and most established families of Williamsburg annually contribute this $1,000 to the church. Are the contributions deductible as charitable contributions?

2. Big Sports University regularly sells out the tickets to its football games. Contributors of $10,000 or more to the athletic scholarship fund are given first choice to purchase two 50-yard-line season tickets for $600. The face value of each season ticket book is $300, but the fair market value of these tickets on the secondary market is $3,000. Is the contribution to the BSU scholarship fund a deductible charitable contribution under § 170?

3. (a) Elijah Craig is a supporter of the Kentucky Museum of Bourbon, a public charity exempt from tax under § 501(c)(3). This year he donated to the Museum an antique Louisville Slugger baseball bat that he had purchased several years ago for investment purposes. Elijah had acquired the baseball bat for $6,000, and had recently been offered $15,000 for it by an antique dealer. The Museum immediately sold the baseball bat at auction for $25,000 and used the proceeds to purchase antique distilling equipment. Assuming that Elijah would have had long-term capital gain had he sold the baseball bat, what are the tax consequences to him from the contribution?

   (b) What would be the amount of Elijah's deduction if he had instead donated to the Museum of Bourbon antique distilling equipment that would be displayed in the museum?

   (c) What would be the amount of Elijah's deduction if he had instead donated to the Museum of Bourbon 100 shares of stock in Corn Products Corporation, which he purchased as an investment many years ago for $6,000, which were now worth $15,000, and which the Museum promptly sold?

4. Darrell Developer donated to the City School District a one-acre parcel of land in the middle of a subdivision that Darrell is developing. The parcel will be used for an elementary school to be built by the District. The land cost Darrell $2,000 and its fair market value currently is $10,000. Can Darrell claim a charitable contribution, and if so, in what amount?

5. Leland Lawyer prepared articles of incorporation and bylaws for the Haight-Ashbury Neighborhood radio station and obtained a tax-exemption for the corporation as a public charity. Leland normally charges $5,000 for preparing articles and bylaws and obtaining a tax-exemption, but formed the radio

station as an act of community service, not billing for his services. Is Leland entitled to a charitable contribution deduction for the value of his services?

6. Clinton Tyree owned a parcel of undeveloped wetlands that he purchased as an investment several years ago for $80,000. The land was recently appraised at $200,000. Clinton sold the land to the Florida chapter of the Nature Conservancy for $150,000, intending to make a charitable contribution of the difference between the value of the property and the sale price. What are the tax consequences to Clinton of the sale?

7. Jeff Thomas transferred his tobacco farm to the University of Central Virginia for eventual use for agricultural teaching and research. Jeff reserved a life estate in the farm. The remainder interest is valued at $50,000. Is Jeff entitled to a charitable contribution deduction?

SECTION 4. STATE AND LOCAL TAXES

1. (a)(i) Mr. and Mrs. Welloff purchased a home in College Town for their daughter Penelope, who is enrolled at the College Town University, to live in while she was attending CTU. Mr. and Mrs. Welloff paid the $3,500 property tax bill on the house. May they deduct the property taxes?

(a)(ii) Would your answer change if Mr. and Mrs. Welloff transferred title to the home to Penelope, and because they are putting Penelope through school, Mr. and Mrs. Welloff paid the $3,500 property tax bill assessed against Penelope?

(b) Mr. and Mrs. Welloff, who owned the house, also paid the annual $480 waste collection charge, which is assessed on a parcel-by-parcel basis. May they deduct the waste collection charge?

(c) The city assessed Mr. and Mrs. Welloff $1,000 for the installation of a water meter on the water line to the house. They paid the assessment. May they deduct the $1,000 as a tax?

2. (a) Florida imposes a sales tax, but has no income tax. Montana has no sales tax but imposes an income tax on residents. Last year, Mike, who lives in Florida, paid $4,000 of sales tax. Ike, who lives in Montana, paid $4,000 of income tax. May Mike and Ike deduct their state taxes?

(b) Would your answer to Part (a), above, change if Mike lived in New Jersey, which imposes both an income tax and a sales tax, Mike's New Jersey income tax liability were $9,000, and Mike had paid $2,400 in sales taxes on the purchase of a new car, $2,000 in sales taxes on the purchase of a new Steinway piano, and $6,000 in sales taxes on all of his other purchases?

SECTION 5. QUALIFIED HOME MORTGAGE INTEREST

1. Drew purchased a 38-foot motor home for $90,000. Drew paid $15,000 in cash and borrowed the remaining $75,000 of the purchase price from the Third National Bank. The loan was secured by the motor home. This year Drew paid $4,000 of interest on the motor home loan. Drew already has a purchase money mortgage of $150,000 on her permanent residence in Buffalo. Is the interest on the motor home loan deductible? Does it matter whether Drew, who spends most of the year living in Buffalo, uses the motor home to spend the winter in Florida, or only for brief camping trips?

2. (a) Patrick owns and lives in a house the fair market value of which is $250,000 and which is subject to a mortgage of $100,000. Patrick borrows an additional $40,000, secured by a second mortgage on the house. He uses the loan proceeds to purchase a new car for his personal (nonbusiness) use. Patrick pays $2,400 of interest in the current year on the $40,000 loan. May Patrick deduct this interest?

   (b) Instead of the automobile, Patrick uses the loan proceeds to purchase stocks and bonds. During the year Patrick has $2,000 of interest and dividends that are included in his gross income. To what extent may Patrick deduct the interest?

   (c) Instead, Patrick uses the $40,000 loan proceeds to purchase tax-exempt municipal bonds. May Patrick deduct the $2,400 of interest?

SECTION 6. CASUALTY LOSSES

1. (a) Noah's adjusted gross income for the year (from his animal husbandry activities) is $100,000. After a tropical rainstorm that lasted 40 days, the contents of Noah's house were partially destroyed by flooding. The damaged property had a basis of $40,000, and Noah suffered a $20,000 loss on this property as a result of the flood. Assuming the property was uninsured, how much of Noah's $20,000 loss is deductible?

   (b) Assuming instead that Noah's property was insured up to $5,000, how much of the loss is deductible?

2. (a) A wave of thefts swept through Ruth's neighborhood last year. In March, Ruth's apartment was burglarized, and her coin collection, valued at $15,000 was stolen. The coins, which were never recovered, had a basis of only $3,000. Ruth's insurance coverage was limited to $5,000. In July, Ruth's jet ski and its trailer were stolen and were never recovered. The jet ski and trailer had a basis of $7,000, a fair market value of $2,000, and were not insured for theft loss. Ruth's adjusted gross income for the year was $50,000. What is the amount of her casualty loss deduction?

(b) Would your answer be different if the fair market value of the jet ski and trailer were $8,000?

SECTION 7. LIMITATIONS ON ITEMIZED DEDUCTIONS

1. Dina earned $200,000 as an associate at a large Boston consulting firm. At her employer's recommendation, Dina took a year-long course in Corporate Strategy at the Harvard Business School, while continuing to work for the firm. The course cost Dina $14,000, and she was not reimbursed for her expenses. Assuming that this expense qualifies for deduction under § 162, how do § 67 and § 68 affect Dina's deduction, assuming that Dina has no other deductible expenses? [For purposes of this problem, you should ignore the adjustments for inflation, and use $100,000 as the "applicable amount" in § 68].

CHAPTER 22

STANDARD DEDUCTION, PERSONAL AND DEPENDENCY EXEMPTIONS, AND PERSONAL CREDITS

SECTION 1. PERSONAL EXEMPTIONS AND THE STANDARD DEDUCTION

1. Jose and Maria Lopez file a joint return as married individuals. Jose and Maria's adjusted gross income for the current year is $60,000. They live in Florida, a state without an income tax, do not own a home, and give little to charity. Mario and Carmen Hernandez are also married taxpayers who file a joint return. They also live in Florida, do not own a home, and give little to charity. Mario and Carmen also had $60,000 of adjusted gross income last year. Mario required surgery during the year, which cost $10,000 but which is deductible under § 213 because he is uninsured and paid for the surgery himself. Assuming neither couple incurred any other deductible expenses, will either couple elect to itemize or will they claim the standard deduction for the year? Why or why not? Do the couples differ significantly in the amount of their tax liability for the year? Should they? Do they differ with respect to the amount of disposable income available for discretionary consumption?

2. (a) Ben files his tax return as an unmarried individual. His gross income for the year consisted of $100,000 of investment income. During the year Ben incurred $20,000 of investment expenses that are deductible under § 212. Ben has no other income or deductions. What is Ben's taxable income?

   (b) Jerry, an unmarried individual, is the sole proprietor of an ice cream shop. Jerry derived $100,000 of gross income from his business and incurred $20,000 of business expenses that are deductible under § 162. Jerry had no other income or deductions for the year. What is Jerry's taxable income?

3. What is the total amount of personal and dependency exemptions in each of the following situations?

(a) Jimmy is single, lives alone, and his AGI is $300,000.

(b) Jessica and Ray are newlyweds who will now file a joint return. Their combined AGI is $550,000.

(c) Phil is divorced with two small children who live with him and who he is entitled to claim as dependents. His AGI is $295,000.

4. (a) Rosencrantz and his wife have six dependent children. Guildenstern and his wife have none. If both families have AGI of $250,000 and considering only the personal and dependency exemptions, how will their taxable incomes differ? Does your answer change if the families have AGI of $500,000 each?

(b) In the case of the Rosencrantz and Guildenstern families, what is the explicit marginal tax rate on taxable income above $420,000 and what is the effective marginal rate faced by each couple if they have $450,000 of AGI? Are these tax rates appropriate?

5. Lance and Kim file a joint return, although Kim earns all of the income reported on the return. May they claim a dependency exemption for their children under the following circumstances?

(a) Their son Chris is 21 years old and a full-time college student at East South Central State University ("ESCSU"). He earned $6,000 last year and used that to pay college expenses. Lance and Kim contributed another $6,000 toward Chris's college expenses and provided him with free room and board at home during the summer.

(b) The facts are the same as in part (a), except that Chris earned $10,000 last year, which he used to buy a used car and pay 50 percent of his college expenses.

(c) The facts are the same as in part (a), except that Chris earned only $4,000, which he used to buy a used car, and he received a $6,000 scholarship from ESCSU.

(d) The facts are the same as in part (a), except that Chris also borrowed $6,000 from ESCSU to pay part of his college expenses.

(e) Lance and Kim have a daughter Ashley, who is 19 years old and graduated from high school in June. From June to December, she traveled through South America on a trip paid for by Lance and Kim. On December 31, she married Ulysses, and they filed a joint return.

6. Archie totally supports numerous members of his extended family. With respect to which of the following may he claim a dependency exemption?

(a) His aunt, who has no income and lives in an apartment for which Archie pays the rent.

(b) His cousin Sheila and her son, who have no income and live in an apartment for which Archie pays the rent.

(c) Same as part (b), except that they live in Archie's house.

(d) Same as part (c), except that Sheila earned $2,000 selling pottery at craft shows.

7. Grandma Moses is 93 years old and lives in an extended care facility. She has no income and is entirely supported by her Daughter, Grandson, and Granddaughter. Daughter and Grandson each provide 40 percent of Grandma's support; Granddaughter provides 20 percent of Grandma's support. Who may claim a dependency exemption for Grandma?

8. (a) Jenn and Ben were divorced last year. They have two minor children, Holly and Nick. Holly spends eight months with Jenn and four months with Ben each year; Nick lives with Ben for eight months and Jenn for four months each year. Ben provides $9,000 to support each child every year; Jenn provides $8,000 to support each child every year. Jenn's mother provides $1,000 for each child each year. If the divorce agreement is silent on the question of dependency exemptions for the children, who is entitled to a dependency exemption for Nick and for Holly?

(b) May Jenn and Ben allocate the dependency exemption by agreement?

(c) If Holly turns 18, goes to college, has no income, and spends only two months of the year with Jenn and one month with Ben, who will be entitled to the dependency exemption if the divorce agreement is silent and:

(i) Jenn provides over 50 percent of Holly's support?

(ii) Ben provides over 50 percent of Holly's support?

(iii) Grandpa provides 60 percent of Holly's support for the year by paying most of her educational expenses, and Jenn and Ben each contribute 20 percent of Holly's support for the year?

SECTION 2. PERSONAL CREDITS

1. Kayla is an unmarried law student with no dependents. Her only income for last year was $5,000 from her summer job with a law firm. Is Kayla entitled to an earned income tax credit for last year? Do you need more information to decide?

2. (a) Miranda is a single mother with two children, ages 5 and 8. She has a 20-hour per week job that pays her $10,000 per year. Miranda has been offered a full time job that pays $20,000 per year. Accepting that job will increase her child care expenses by $50 per week, or approximately $2,500 per year. What is the impact on her earned income credit if Miranda takes the full-time job?

    (b) Miranda keeps the 20-hour per week job and has a third child. What is the effect of that on the amount of her earned income tax credit?

3. The Internal Revenue Service is auditing the tip income of waiters and waitresses at the Truckee Diner, home of excellent hamburgers and milkshakes. The revenue agent discovers that Maggie, who earns $2,000 in hourly wages as a waitress, reports $8,000 in tips. All of the other waiters and waitresses report tip income no greater than 200 percent of their salaries. Is Maggie unusually honest, or should the agent suspect something else is going on?

4. Dan has asked Roseanne to marry him. Dan and Roseanne each earn about $15,000 per year. Roseanne has two children, as does Dan. Purely from a federal income tax perspective, is marriage a good financial deal for Dan and Roseanne?

5. You serve on the staff of James Madison, a member of the House Ways and Means Committee. He has asked you to analyze the merits of a bill to repeal I.R.C. § 21, which grants a credit for certain dependent care expenses, and in its place to enact new I.R.C. § 162(a)(4), which would specifically describe such expenses as expenses paid or incurred in carrying on a trade or business. Representative Madison is particularly interested in knowing whether the proposed legislation would move the law closer to or further from the theoretically correct treatment of such expenses as compared with current law. What do you tell him?

6. Scott and Zelda are married and have two children, twin boys who are 6 years old. Scott and Zelda are both newspaper reporters and each earned $70,000 last year. They had no other gross income and their AGI was $140,000. Their work schedules are erratic, so a day care center, which would have cost about $8,000 was not an option for them because neither could reliably be available

to pick the boys up from daycare. Scott and Zelda therefore hired a nanny to care for the children until one of the parents was able to get home and paid the nanny $25,000 per year (including applicable employment taxes). The nanny also prepared meals, did the children's laundry and tided up the house. Can Scott and Zelda claim any portion of the amounts they paid the nanny and incurred as a result of employing her as a child care credit last year? If so, how much?

CHAPTER 23

TAX EXPENDITURES FOR EDUCATION

1. You are a legislative assistant to Tom Jefferson, a State Senator who sits on the Education Committee of the Virginia legislature. Funds for public higher education are tight but pressure to keep down tuition is intense. You learn of the federal Hope and Lifetime Learning credits. What can you advise Senator Jefferson that will help him out of the spot he is in?

2. Senator Jefferson asks you why the federal deduction for qualified higher education expenses is allowed against gross income rather than as an itemized personal deduction allowable only against adjusted gross income. What do you tell him?

3. Homer wants to help with the higher education expenses for his grandchildren. He is thinking about just putting the money in a savings account and letting it build up until they enter college. Does Homer have better options?

PART VI

Characterization of Gains and Losses

CHAPTER 24

Capital Gains and Losses

SECTION 1. SPECIAL TREATMENT OF CAPITAL GAINS AND LOSSES

1. In each of the following cases, how much net capital gain does the taxpayer have according to § 1222? If the taxpayer has an amount in addition to or instead of net capital gain, how is that other amount taxed?

(a) The taxpayer has $1,000 of long-term-capital gain.

(b) The taxpayer has $1,000 of long-term capital loss.

(c) The taxpayer has $1,000 of long-term capital gain and $2,000 of short-term capital gain.

(d) The taxpayer has $1,000 of short-term capital gain and $1,000 of short-term capital loss.

(e) The taxpayer has $1,000 of long-term capital gain, $2,000 of short-term capital gain and $1,000 of short-term capital loss.

(f) The taxpayer has $1,000 of long-term capital gain, $1,000 of short-term capital gain, and $2,000 of short-term capital loss.

(g) The taxpayer has $5,000 of long-term capital gain, $1,000 of long-term capital loss, $1,000 of short-term capital gain, and $3,000 of short-term capital loss.

(h) The taxpayer has $3,000 of long-term capital gain, $1,000 of long-term capital loss, $1,000 of short-term capital gain and $5,000 of short-term capital loss.

2. Cap is an unmarried individual who has $220,000 of taxable income. Cap's taxable income includes salary of $170,000, $20,000 of gain from the sale of stock that Cap had held for more than one year, $40,000 of gain from the sale of stock held for less than one year, $30,000 of losses from stock held for less than one year, $15,000 of gain from the sale of rental real estate which Cap purchased for $150,000 and sold for $140,000. Cap claimed $25,000 of depreciation deductions during the six years he held the real estate for the production of income. Cap also had $5,000 of gain from the sale of a painting he purchased several years ago. Applying the formula of § 1(h), calculate Cap's tax liability.

SECTION 2. DEFINITION OF "CAPITAL ASSET"

A. THE STATUTORY EXCLUSIONS

(1) INVESTMENT PROPERTY VERSUS PROPERTY HELD FOR SALE TO CUSTOMERS

1. Samantha Subdivider purchased Kirkwood Acres, a 1,000 acre parcel of land, for $1,000,000. Samantha spent $200,000 installing sewer lines and subdividing the land into 250 quarter-acre parcels. For the next couple of years Samantha devoted her efforts to selling home sites on other properties that she had developed. Three years ago Samantha sold 150 home sites at Kirkwood Acres. Samantha then deferred further sales efforts thinking that the remaining land would appreciate substantially over the next few years. For the last two years

Samantha was engaged in developing apartment complexes for Boxed Homes Construction. In the current year, Boxed Homes entered into a deal with Samantha to purchase the remaining land at Kirkwood Acres for construction of a single apartment complex. Will Samantha be able to claim capital gains treatment on the sale of the Kirkwood Acres parcels?

2. Pam Prof is a professor in the Business School at Enormous State University. Her annual salary from ESU is $150,000. Believing that she should practice what she preaches, Pam is a real estate investor on the side. Over the years Pam has acquired a large number of rental properties. Presently she owns almost sixty rental units, most of which are duplexes or four-plexes, but some of which are single-family homes. Pam specializes in renting to married graduate students at ESU because they tend to do less damage to the rental units. When a particular rental unit becomes too shabby to attract the class of graduate students that Pam prefers as tenants, Pam sells the property to someone who specializes in leasing properties to undergraduates. The key factor in making the decision when to sell is whether or not Pam expects to maximize the selling price by selling at that time. In any particular year, Pam usually sells three or four of her properties and replaces them with new properties. In the past five years, Pam's average profits from real estate rentals have been $100,000 and she has averaged $90,000 of aggregate gains on the sales of the properties. Are Pam's gains from buying and selling homes eligible for capital gains treatment?

3. Mike Millkem earns all of his income from his substantial investment activities. His annual interest and dividend income exceeds $300,000. In addition, Mike regularly buys and sells shares of portfolio stock in an attempt to derive gains from short-term profit swings. Mike's purchase and sales activity includes investments in the options market. Mike's investment activities require his full-time attention. Last year Mike made 300 purchases at an aggregate price of $4,000,000 and sales at an aggregate price of $3,800,000. May Mike deduct his $200,000 net loss as an ordinary loss?

4. Pat Poultry purchased a 500-acre tract adjacent to her world famous Poultry-in-Motion free-range chicken ranch several years ago for $800,000, borrowing $700,000 from BigOne Bank to finance the purchase. Pat expanded the chicken ranch over 350 acres, but left the 150 acres farthest from the existing operations as a buffer against encroaching subdivisions and commercial development to protect her chickens from the noise and pollution. Earlier this year, Pat fell behind on her loan payments, and BigOne Bank, which held a mortgage to secure the $700,000 loan to finance the purchase, suggested to Pat that she subdivide and sell some of the 500 acres to start to pay down the loan. Since some of the land on the farthest side of the new tract was too hilly, rocky, and wooded to be cost effectively converted to free range chicken

farming, Pat agreed. Pat obtained subdivision approval for ten 5-acre "mini-ranchette" lots and thereafter sold all ten lots through a local real estate broker. Pat cleared a total of $500,000 on the lots (after broker's commissions) and realized an aggregate gain of $420,000 on the land sales. May Pat report these gains as capital gains? Is your answer affected by how much Pat typically makes from her free range chicken farming activity?

(2)   SECTION 1221(a)(2): REAL PROPERTY AND DEPRECIABLE PROPERTY HELD FOR USE IN THE TAXPAYER'S TRADE OR BUSINESS

1. Stains-R-Us Dry Cleaners recently sold its dry-cleaning plant property to Toxins-R-Us Chemical Manufacturing Company. The basis of the land was $1,000,000 and the basis of the building was $1,500,000. Because of the immense environmental remediation issues, Toxins paid Stains-R-Us only $300,000 for the land and $200,000 for the building. Are Stains-R-Us's losses capital losses?

(3) SECTION 1221(a)(3): INVESTMENT PROFITS VERSUS REWARD FOR PERSONAL SERVICES

1. While browsing through the voluminous pile of catalogs that fill his mailbox every day, many of them featuring clothing with various logos, Neal LaHeat was struck by the idea that basketball players would like a line of shorts emblazoned with a design of a genii. After some negotiations that lasted more than one year, Neal sold his ideas to SellaLogo, a major catalog / internet sports apparel vendor, which registered the genii logo as a trademark. May Neal treat the $500,000 he received from SellaLogo as a long-term capital gain?

2. (a) Orlando Martin is a professional bass fisherman who invented a revolutionary new bass-fishing boat trolling motor control mechanism in his spare time after encountering practical problems with all existing control mechanisms. Orlando secured a patent on the new trolling motor.

   (i) If Orlando sells the patent to BassMaster Shops, Inc., the nation's largest fishing equipment manufacturer, for $10,000,000, does Orlando realize capital gain?

   (ii) If Orlando gives BassMaster Shops, Inc. an exclusive license to exploit the patent in exchange for a royalty of one percent of gross sales, and over the life of the patent Orlando receives royalties of $15,000,000 from BassMaster, does Orlando realize capital gain or ordinary income?

3. Alvin Edison is a professional inventor who holds over 100 patents on computer hardware components. Alvin recently secured a patent on a chip that is 100 times faster and half the size of the next best chip.

(a) If Alvin sells the patent to Worldwide Business Machines, the world's largest computer manufacturer, for $50,000,000, does Alvin realize capital gain?

(b) If Alvin gives Worldwide an exclusive license to exploit the patent in exchange for a royalty of one percent of gross sales, and over the life of the patent Alvin receives royalties of $30,000,000 from Worldwide, does Alvin realize capital gain?

(c) Does your answer change if Alvin's license to Worldwide was limited to sales of computers everywhere in the world but Asia, and Alvin retained the right to exploit the patent in Asia?

4. (a) Eric King had owned and operated King's Instruments for 40 years before he retired last year. Just before his retirement, his major competitor, Clapton's Guitars, offered King $250,000 for the right to use King's name. Clapton wanted to rename his store King and Clapton's Instruments to attract King's many loyal customers to Clapton's shop. King had no obligation to perform any services. May King treat the $250,000 as long-term capital gain?

(b) If King had died while operating the shop and Clapton had paid King's widow, Lucille, $250,000 for the right to use King's name, could Lucille treat the amount as long-term capital gain?

(7) SECTION 1221(a)(7): HEDGING TRANSACTIONS

1. Shrub & Sons, Inc., the nation's largest producer of deep-fried pork rinds, and just plain pork, purchases millions of pounds of pork annually. To minimize pre-processing inventory storage costs, it purchases hogs only a few weeks before they will be processed. This results in a significant risk to Shrub & Sons of an inadequate supply of pork and/or large and sudden increases in the price of hogs. In order to minimize this risk, Shrub & Sons regularly enters into pork futures contracts, requiring it to buy a specified quantity of pork at a specified price at a specified date in the future. Although Shrub & Sons sometimes takes delivery under these contracts, most often it sells the contracts shortly before the specified date and simply buys the hogs it needs on the market. If the price of hogs has risen, it sells the contracts at a gain that offsets the increased price it must pay for hogs. Conversely, if the price of hogs falls, it sells the futures contracts at a loss, and the loss offsets the savings

from the decrease in the price it pays for hogs. Are the gains and losses on the sales of the pork futures contracts ordinary or capital?

2. Sulphuric Electric Power Corporation is a large midwestern electric company. For many years it has operated a number of coal powered electric generating plants. To assure that it would have all of the low-cost coal that it required in the event of the resurgence of inflation, another energy crisis, or other national emergency, Sulphuric purchased an 80 percent controlling interest in Acid-Runoff Mining Corp., which operated a large low-cost coal mine in Wyoming. Recently, with a changing political climate, Sulphuric has decided that the risks with which it was concerned when it purchased the stock of Acid-Runoff no longer exist and that its resources would be more profitably invested in trading electricity futures in the deregulated Texas market. To that end it sold the Acid-Runoff stock and realized a $100,000,000 loss. May Sulphuric deduct the loss as an ordinary loss or is it a capital loss?

(8) SECTION 1221(a)(8): NON-INVENTORY SUPPLIES

1. Hospital Corporation of the Nation (HCN) operates the largest chain of for-profit hospitals in the country. It annually purchases tens of millions of dollars worth of bandages, bedpans, paper cups, over-the-counter drugs, and other medical supplies for day-to-day use in treating patients. HCN usually attempts to keep a 30-day supply of all such items on hand. Recently, HCN discovered that due to a computer virus that had infected its purchasing software it had inadvertently purchased a 90-day supply of most of these items. To minimize carrying costs, HCN sold half of what it had on hand to Suwannee Old Folks Homes, Inc., the nation's largest nursing home chain. Is the gain or loss HCN realized on the sale of the bandages, bedpans, paper cups, over-the-counter drugs, and other medical supplies ordinary or capital?

B. JUDICIAL LIMITATIONS ON CAPITAL ASSET CLASSIFICATION

1. (a) Several years ago, Will leased an entire office building to Doorway Computer Corp. for a term of 25 years, for an annual rent of $50,000. If Will assigns the annual rents due under the remaining term of the lease to Allen for $400,000, may Will treat that amount as long-term capital gain?

(b) If, one year later, Allen sold to Karen for $410,000 the right to the rentals that he purchased in part (a), may Allen treat his gain as long-term capital gain?

(c) If Will sells an undivided half interest in the building for $300,000, must Will treat $200,000 (half of the present value of the rentals) as ordinary income and only $100,000 as the amount realized on the sale of the interest in the building?

(d) If Will pays Doorway Computer Corp. $350,000 to surrender its lease, which has 20 more years to run, may Doorway Computer Corp. treat that amount as long-term capital gain?

(e) If Doorway Computer Corp. had sublet the building to Packard Automobile Corp. three years ago for $55,000 a year, and later, Packard Automobile Corp. paid Doorway Computer Corp. $34,000 for an assignment of all of Doorway Computer Corp.'s interest in the lease, could Doorway Computer Corp. have treated that amount as long-term capital gain?

2. For many years Michael Hewlett operated a computer repair and servicing company named Dog Bytes. As part of the Dog Bytes business, Michael had a contract with the State University System to service all of the personal computers used in the university system. The contract, which had a five year term, was entered into 18 months ago and provides for a guaranteed minimum payment to Dog Bytes of $250,000 per year. If Michael sells the Dog Bytes business, including the State University System contract (which is assignable) to Steven Tasks, and Michael and Steven validly agree that $400,000 of the overall purchase is allocable to the State University System contract, does Michael recognize ordinary income or capital gain with respect to the contract?

SECTION 3. SALE OR EXCHANGE REQUIREMENT

A. TERMINATION OF TAXPAYER'S INTEREST WITHOUT A "TRANSFER"—THE CREDITOR'S SITUATION

1. John Mellon Carnegie died many years ago, leaving his $100 million estate in trust, with the income to be paid equally among his children for the rest of their lives, and the remainder to be divided equally among his grandchildren upon the death of his last surviving child. In addition, each child was entitled to $10,000,000 in cash or property from the corpus 20 years after John's death. Several years ago, Carl Iconic paid John's son Andrew $7,000,000 for Andrew's right to the $10,000,000 distribution. This year, the trust satisfied the obligation by distributing $10,000,000 in cash to Carl. Does Carl recognize ordinary income or capital gain? How much?

2. Jack entered into a contract to sell his opulent vacation home in Palm Beach to Dennis for $25,000,000. Dennis made an "earnest money" down payment of $500,000. When soon thereafter Dennis lost his job as president of ToyCo Corporation, he defaulted on the purchase and sale agreement, and the deposit

was forfeited to Jack. Does Jack recognize ordinary income or capital gain as result of receipt of the forfeited down payment?

3. In November of last year, Ariel bought 400 shares of stock in Mermaid Cruise Lines, Inc. for $10,000. On April 1 of the current year, she sold 200 shares, in which she had a basis of $5,000, for $1,000. On April 2, Mermaid Cruise Lines went into receivership. By June 1 it was clear that the common shareholders of Mermaid Cruise Lines would receive nothing from the bankruptcy estate. What is the character of Ariel's losses from these events?

4. Jerry Robertson invested $100,000 in a partnership that set out to make a movie about the life of Johnny Appleseed. Subsequently the managing partners decided there was not much of a market for a film biography of Johnny Appleseed and they rewrote the plot, hired new actors, renamed the movie, "Really Bad Appleseeds," and produced a pornographic movie. Jerry's sensibilities were so offended by the production of a pornographic movie that he simply walked away from the partnership, even declining to sue to get his invested money back because it was, in his words, "tainted." May Jerry deduct his $100,000 basis in the abandoned partnership interest as an ordinary loss?

SECTION 4. HOLDING PERIOD REQUIREMENT

1. Howard Cunningham, a cash-method taxpayer, bought and sold stock in the following transactions. What are the amount and character of his gain or loss in each case?

   (a) On July 31 of last year, Howard purchased 200 shares of stock in HomeDepot for $10,000. He sold the shares on July 31 of this year for $12,000.

   (b) On August 31 of last year, Howard purchased 200 shares of HomeDepot stock for $10,000. He sold the shares on September 1 of this year for $9,000.

   (c) Four years ago, Howard purchased 100 shares of HomeDepot stock for $8,000. In November of last year, he purchased another 100 shares for $13,000. In August of this year, he ordered his broker to sell 100 shares for $10,000, and the broker executed the order.

2. (a) On July 1 of last year, Ravi purchased 500 shares of stock in General Motors for $10,000. In May of this year, when the fair market value of the stock was $9,000, he gave the stock to his daughter, Norah. Norah sold the stock in August. What would be the amount and character of her gain if Norah sold the stock for $11,000?

(b) What would be the amount and character of Norah's loss if she sold the stock for $8,000?

3. Nat purchased 200 shares of stock in Jazz Piano Mfg. Corp. for $1,000 on August 1. On November 1, when the stock was worth $1,300, Nat died. The following January his executor sold the Jazz Piano Mfg. Corp. stock for $1,500. What is the character of the gain recognized by the estate?

4. Danny Simons paid $5,000 to purchase a used, fairly decrepit 32-foot racing sloop at a boat yard on San Pablo Bay last year. He named the boat "Sgt. Shultz." Last year, he spent countless hours and $3,000 for materials trying to get the boat in shape for ocean racing, but the task was far from completed. Nevertheless, so much had been accomplished that around the New Year Denny O'Connor offered Danny $15,000 for the Sgt. Shultz. Still planning to finish the restoration and race the Sgt. Shultz to Hawaii, Danny declined the offer. This year, Danny finished the restoration, spending an additional $4,000. This year, Danny decided he would rather become a professional skier than continue as an amateur sailboat racer, and sold the Sgt. Shultz to O'Connor for $40,000. What is the character of Danny's gain?

SECTION 5. SPECIAL STATUTORY TREATMENT OF PARTICULAR GAINS AND LOSSES

1. (a) John Elton paid Elvis Holly $5,000 for an option to purchase Dreamland Acres (a parcel of undeveloped land) for $100,000 at any time during the next 12 months. The value of Dreamland Acres never exceeded $90,000 during the option period, so John failed to exercise the option. If John had exercised the option, he would have held Dreamland Acres for speculative investment. May John treat the $5,000 cost of the option as an ordinary loss?

(b) How should Elvis treat the $5,000 he received from John for the option?

SECTION 6. TRANSACTIONAL PROBLEMS OF CAPITAL GAINS AND LOSSES

1. (a) Chip Spam, a computer wizard graduate of State Institute of Technology, started a new computer company, BigBytes. Chip raised money from a venture capitalist, RRK partnership, by selling RRK a $10,000,000 convertible debenture. Eventually, BigBytes went public, Chip cashed out and invested his $20,000,000 sales proceeds in a diversified portfolio and RRK converted its debenture into common stock of BigBytes, hoping that eventually MacroSoft,

the world's largest computer company, would make a generous takeover offer. Chip reported a capital gain of over $19,000,000. Not only did MacroSoft never make an offer, but soon thereafter BigBytes business was virtually nonexistent, as the purported advanced technology on which Chip's initial investment had been made and the company had been taken public was significantly exaggerated. RRK sued Chip seeking damages for common law fraud and violation of the federal securities laws in connection with the sale. Chip settled by paying RRK $10,000,000. Does Chip recognize an ordinary loss or a capital loss as a result of making this payment?

(b) The year after Chip cashed out of BigBytes, the company's counsel informed him that his sale of BigBytes stock violated Section 16(b) of the Securities Exchange Act and Chip made the payment required under that statute. Would Chip be correct in treating that payment as an ordinary and necessary business expense deductible under § 162?

2. Last year Chet sold some equipment that he had is his business as a free-lance landscape photographer. He recognized losses of $10,000 on the sale, and since those were his only § 1231 transactions during that year, he properly treated the losses as ordinary losses. Chet had sued the manufacturer of the equipment on the ground that the equipment was defective, and this year he recovered $7,000 in damages from the manufacturer. Is the recovery capital gain or ordinary income?

4. Shelly owns several parcels of vacant land that she bought several years ago with funds borrowed from Monolith Bank. She properly deducted the interest on the loans (she had other investment income), and this year sold the parcels for a gain of $150,000. Is the gain ordinary or capital?

CHAPTER 25

SALES OF ASSETS HELD FOR USE IN A TRADE OR BUSINESS

SECTION 1. SECTION 1231 PROPERTY

1. (a) Jack L. Hyde owns several small office buildings in which he rents space to doctors, dentists, lawyers, and other professionals. Last year he sold two of his rental buildings. Hyde sold one building, Doctors' Park, in which his basis was $400,000, for $450,000. Hyde sold the second building, Lawyers' Tower, for $470,000. Hyde's basis in Lawyers' Tower was $540,000. He had owned both buildings for several years. What is the character of Hyde's gain and loss?

(b) How does the answer change if Hyde's basis in Lawyers' Tower, which he sold for $470,000, was $490,000?

(c) How does the answer to part (a) change if Hyde's basis in Doctors' Park was $490,000?

(d)(i) How would your answer to part (a) change if Hyde sold Doctors' Park last year and sold Lawyers' Tower this year?

   (ii) How would your answer to part (a) change if Hyde sold Lawyers' Tower last year and sold Doctors' Park this year?

(e) What would have been the character of the gain and loss in (b) if Doctors' Park had been held for only 11 months?

2. Last year Michelle sold for $40,000 an unimproved tract of land, in which she had a basis of $50,000. Michelle had been leasing the land to a lobster fisher who used it to assemble and repair lobster traps. Also last year another unimproved tract of land Michelle held for speculative purposes and in which she had a basis of $20,000 and a holding period of more than one year was condemned by the state for a road project, and Michelle received $26,000. In addition, the bank in which Michelle had a safe deposit box was burglarized and numismatic coins which had cost her $3,000 and which she had held for speculative investment for several years were taken. Michelle received $12,000

of insurance proceeds for the theft from the safe deposit box. What is the character of Michelle's gains and losses arising from these events?

3. Fly-by-Night Corp. operates an overnight air courier service. Several years ago, Fly-by-Night purchased a Boeing 737 airplane for $50,000,000. During the period it operated the airplane, Fly-by-Night claimed $30,000,000 of depreciation deductions. If that is the only § 1231 property Fly-by-Night sold that year, what is the character of Fly-by-Night's gain or loss if it sold the airplane for each of the following amounts?

   (a) $25,000,000?

   (b) $55,000,000?

   (c) $15,000,000?

4. When Studebaker Automobile Mfg. Co. went out of business a few years ago, Packard Corp, a start-up automobile company, purchased from Studebaker's bankruptcy estate for $1,500,000 the trade name "Studebaker Avanti." Since then, Packard has properly claimed $400,000 of amortization deductions under § 197 with respect to the trade name. This year Packard sold the Studebaker Avanti trade name to DeSoto Motors. If that is the only § 1231 property Packard sold that year, what is the character of Packard's gain or loss if it sold the trade name for each of the following amounts:

   (a) $2,000,000?

   (b) $1,300,000?

   (c) $900,000?

5. Last year, Rita Rental sold one of several office buildings that he owned. Rita Rental received $800,000 for the building. Of this amount $450,000 was attributable to the building and the remaining $350,000 was attributable to the land. Rita Rental had purchased the building for $500,000 in 1988; $100,000 of the purchase price was attributable to the land, and $400,000 had been attributable to the building. Over the period that he operated the building, Rita Rental claimed $155,000 of depreciation deductions. Rita Rental's ordinary income is subject to tax at the 36 percent marginal rate. How much of Rita Rental's gain on the sale of the building will be taxed at the 36 percent rate, 25 percent rate, or 20 percent rate?

6. Charlie Tuna owned a 38-foot offshore fishing boat that he used exclusively in his charter fishing business in the Florida Keys. He paid $300,000 for the boat

several years ago and has properly claimed $250,000 of depreciation deductions. The boat is now worth $190,000.

(a) (i) If Charlie gives the boat to his niece Ariel, will there be any tax consequences to Charlie?

(ii) If Ariel holds the boat solely for personal use for more than a year and then sells it for $195,000, what is the amount and character of her gain?

(b) If Charlie dies when the boat is worth $190,000, Ariel inherits the boat, and after holding it for personal use, Ariel sells the boat for $195,000, what is the amount and character of Ariel's gain?

(c) What are the tax consequences to Charlie if, when the boat is worth $190,000, he gives it to the Sea Explorer Scouts (a charitable organization) for use in scouting activities?

7. Never-on-Time Airlines owned a fully depreciated CRJ regional jet, for which it had originally paid $10,000,000. A few years ago, it obtained a used Boeing 737 from JetOrange&Blue in a § 1031 like-kind exchange in which Never-on-Time gave JetOrange&Blue the CRJ, which was then worth $800,000, and $6,000,000 in cash in exchange for the Boeing 737. Never-on-Time has properly claimed $3,500,000 of depreciation with respect to the 737. This year, because Never-on-Time has been losing business to lower cost discount airlines — like JetOrange&Blue — Never-on-Time sold the Boeing 737 to EastSoutheast Airlines for $13,000,000. What is the character of Never-on-Time's $10,500,000 gain?

8. Polonius's daughter, Ophelia, wishes to enter the plastic skull-making business. She cannot afford a new skull-making machine, but Polonius sells her one of his used skull-making machines for $12,000, which he knows to be $8,000 less than the cost of a new machine ($20,000). Polonius had bought the machine for $10,000 several years ago and properly took depreciation deductions of $5,000. How much income does Polonius recognize as a result of this sale? (Assume that Polonius engages in no other sales of business property during the year.) What is the character of that income? What is Ophelia's basis in the machine? What will be Ophelia's basis for purposes of taking depreciation or cost recovery deductions?

9. (a) Biff Beachbum purchased a beachfront house in Panama City Beach several years ago for $1,000,000; at that time the land was worth $600,000 and the house was worth $400,000. For the last three years, Biff has used the house for vacations. Earlier this year, Biff sold the house to Great Getaways, Inc., in which his wife Missy owns 60 percent of the stock (Missy's brother owns the

other 40 percent), for $2,000,000; at the time of the sale the land was worth $1,200,000, and the house was worth $800,000. Great Getaways, Inc. plans to lease the house on a weekly basis to vacationers in the ordinary course of its business. What is the character of Biff's gain?

(b) Would your answer differ if Missy and her brother each owned 50 percent of the stock of Great Getaways, Inc.?

(c) Would your answer differ if Missy was Biff's granddaughter instead of his wife?

SECTION 2. SALE OF AN ENTIRE BUSINESS

1. Fred Fixit operated a machine shop that made custom parts for old equipment. He had owned the business for 20 years. Recently he sold the unincorporated business operation to I. Gadget for $400,000. The business consisted of the following assets:

Asset	Unadjusted Basis	Adjusted Basis	Value
Accounts Receivable	$60,000	$60,000	$ 50,000
Inventory	$40,000	$40,000	$ 90,000
Machinery	$95,000	$40,000	$ 20,000
Leasehold (5 years remaining on 10 year lease)	$10,000	$ 5,000	$ 20,000
John Moose Power Tool Repair Center Franchise	$15,000	$ 7,000	$ 40,000
Goodwill	$ 0	$ 0	$180,000

(a) What is the amount and character of Fixit's gain?

(b) How would your answer differ if Fixit had purchased the machine shop as a going business from Tim Taylor 15 years ago and Fixit took an unadjusted basis in the goodwill of $50,000 at that time, and at the time of the sale to Gadget, Fixit's goodwill had an adjusted basis of $0 and a fair market value of $130,000.

(c) (i) In addition to the purchase price, Gadget agreed to pay Fixit $20,000 per year for five years for Fixit's agreement not to enter into a manufacturing operation in competition with Gadget. What is the character of Fixit's additional gain?

(ii) How does Gadget treat the additional $100,000 paid to Fixit?

(d) What if Fixit and Gadget allocate only $50,000 to the covenant not to compete ($10,000 per year) but allocate an additional $50,000 to goodwill?

(e) Do the amount and character of gain change if Fixit's operation were incorporated and Fixit sold all of the stock of the business to Gadget for $400,000? Fixit's basis in the stock was $220,000.

PART VII

DEFERRED RECOGNITION OF GAIN FROM PROPERTY

CHAPTER 26

LIKE-KIND EXCHANGES

SECTION 1. LIKE-KIND EXCHANGES IN GENERAL

1. Adam owned undeveloped farmland held as a speculative investment, with a basis of $1,200,000 and a fair market value of $1,800,000. He exchanged the land with Bernice for an apartment complex with a fair market value of $1,800,000. Bernice's basis in the apartment complex is $700,000. Bernice plans to develop an organic ostrich ranch on the farmland to try to profit from the low-carb diet craze.

(a) What is the gain (loss) realized and recognized by Adam and Bernice? What is the basis each of Adam and Bernice has in the property received?

(b) What if the residential rental property transferred by Bernice is worth only $1,500,000 and Bernice also transfers $300,000 of cash to Adam?

(c) In part (b), what if Adam's basis in the farmland is $1,800,000?

(d) In part (b), what if Adam's basis in the farmland is $2,000,000?

(e) What if instead of $300,000 of cash in part (b), Bernice transferred $300,000 of stock in a publicly traded corporation. Bernice's basis in the stock was $400,000.

(f) What if Bernice's basis in the stock transferred in part (e) is $250,000?

2. (a) Charles owns a vacation home at Lake Tahoe with a fair market value of $400,000 and a basis of $150,000. Charles trades the Lake Tahoe home with Davenport for a beachfront house in Virginia Beach with a fair market value of $400,000. Davenport's basis in the beach house is $175,000. Charles and Davenport have used the houses solely as vacation homes and will continue to do so after the exchange. What are the tax consequences to Charles and Davenport on the exchange?

(b) Does the answer change if Charles rents the Lake Tahoe house to tenants before the exchange, and will rent the Virginia Beach house after the exchange? Davenport will use the Lake Tahoe house as a vacation home.

3. Emory transfers land in New York City, with a basis of $60,000, and subject to a mortgage of $50,000, for an interest in an oil and gas lease in New Mexico with a fair market value of $100,000. The transferee assumes Emory's $50,000 liability. What is the gain realized and recognized by Emory? What is Emory's basis in the oil and gas lease?

4. Frances exchanges an apartment building complex, Forestview, with a fair market value of $500,000, subject to a mortgage of $200,000, for Oceanview, an apartment building complex owned by Gayle. The fair market value of Oceanview is $500,000, and it is subject to a mortgage of $250,000. Gayle also transfers $50,000 of cash to Frances. Frances' basis in Forestview is $150,000. Gayle's basis in Oceanview is $100,000. How much gain is realized and recognized by Frances and Gayle? What are Frances' and Gayle's respective bases in the property received by each?

5. (a) Henry Ford owned a large sports utility vehicle (in excess of 6,000 pounds gross vehicle weight) which he uses in his business as an independent contract engineer and bridge designer. Henry's depreciated basis in the vehicle is $3,000. At the local Humpback Whale SUV dealer, Henry trades his vehicle,

which has a NADA Bluebook value of $25,000, plus an additional $40,000 of cash, for a new model with a list price of $65,000. What is Henry's depreciable basis for the new vehicle?

(b) How would your answer change if Henry's basis for his old SUV was $33,000?

(c) Would your answer in part (b) change if Henry sold his old SUV to Humpback Whale SUV for $25,000 on Tuesday and on Wednesday Henry purchased the new SUV for cash?

6. Bernice Baitfish, who has been one of the most successful participants on the female competitive bass fishing tournament tour, has decided to retire from competitive fishing and go into the lure manufacturing business. To that end Bernice traded her legendary (and fully depreciated) bass boat, "Lunker-Geter," to Bass Pro Shops, the nation's leading fishing tackle distributor, for $200,000 worth of lure manufacturing equipment. To what extent can the exchange qualify under § 1031?

7. George, who owns the Bronx Highlanders baseball team in the Coastal Baseball League, and Marge, who owns the Hamilton Red and Blacklegs baseball team in the Heartland Baseball League, want to swap franchises. Each franchise consists primarily of a league affiliation, player contracts, sports equipment (baseballs, bats, uniforms, golf carts to shuttle relief pitchers in from the bull pen, etc.), long term stadium leases, TV and radio contracts, season ticket subscriber lists, and trade names and trademarks. To what extent can the exchange qualify under § 1031?

8. Paul, a highly successful rock musician, has actually made most of his fortune by acquiring, and holding copyrights on works by other artists.for the collection of royalties, To maximize his diversification Paul does not confine his activities to musical compositions. This year Paul exchanged the copyright on three of his songs for three other copyrights. He received back the following: (1) a copyright on a computer video game; (2) a copyright on a novel; and (3) a copyright on a poem. Do any of these exchanges qualify under § 1031?

SECTION 2. MULTIPARTY AND DEFERRED EXCHANGES

1. Gofer Golf wanted to acquire Pat Poultry's famed Poultry in Motion chicken ranch to build a championship golf course on the edge of Expansion City. Pat was hesitant to leave the chicken business and was unwilling to sell unless she could acquire pasture land to preserve her prize free-range chicken herd. Pat's

adjusted basis in the chicken ranch is $125,000. Gofer offered to pay $1,200,000 for the property (excluding the chickens).

(a) Pat Poultry located land owned by Calvin Carnivore that was operated as a cattle ranch, but which was suitable for Pat's chicken operation. Calvin was willing to sell the land for $800,000. Pat agreed to sell her chicken ranch to Gofer for $1,200,000. Pat immediately thereafter purchased the cattle ranch from Calvin for $800,000. What are the tax consequences of this transaction to Pat?

(b) Alternatively, in a single contract entered into on January 2, Gofer Golf agreed to acquire the cattle ranch from Calvin for $800,000. Pat agreed to exchange her chicken ranch with Gofer for the cattle ranch plus $400,000 cash. Gofer deposited $1,200,000 into an escrow account. Pat and Calvin deposited deeds to their respective ranches in the escrow. Escrow closed on June 30. The escrow agent distributed $800,000 cash to Calvin, the deed to Calvin's cattle ranch and $400,000 cash to Pat, and the deed to Pat's chicken farm to Gofer. What are the tax consequences of this arrangement to Pat? What is her basis in the cattle ranch?

(c) What if instead, Pat had not immediately located the suitable replacement property? Pat and Gofer entered into a contract on January 2 under which Gofer transferred $1,200,000 of cash into an escrow account and Pat immediately gave Gofer the deed to her chicken ranch. Under the agreement Pat would locate property suitable for her chicken herd and notify Gofer to acquire the property for transfer to Pat. The agreement also provided that in the event Pat was unable to locate suitable property before February 16, the $1,200,000 deposited in escrow would be distributed to her. The agreement further provided that once identified, Gofer was required to acquire the identified property and transfer the property to Pat on or before June 30. On February 1 Pat discovered Calvin's cattle ranch, which Calvin agreed to sell for $800,000. Pat immediately notified Gofer in writing to acquire Calvin's cattle ranch. Gofer entered into an agreement for the transfer of the cattle ranch through escrow closing on June 30. Calvin deposited the deed to the cattle ranch in the escrow account. On close of escrow, the deed to Calvin's ranch was distributed to Pat along with $400,000 of cash. The remaining $800,000 of cash was distributed to Calvin. What are the tax consequences of this transaction to Pat?

(d) In part (c), would your answer change if Gofer's attorney delivered the final escrow instructions to the agent a couple of days late, and the escrow did not close until July 3?

2. The Newbury News newspaper is planning on expanding from a weekly to five day a week publication. To do so, it needs a new publishing plant. To minimize disruption of its operations, it plans to structure the acquisition as follows. The Newbury News will lend $100,000 to the Williston Title and Abstract Company, which will borrow another $400,000 from the Farmer's and Fisherman's State Bank; the loan will be guaranteed by the Newbury News. Williston Title and Abstract Company will then purchase and improve a building that has been located by the Newbury News, following instructions from an architect hired by Newbury News. When the construction is complete — in about three months — the Williston Title and Abstract Company will deed the property to Newbury News in exchange for its promise to convey the old printing plant to Williston Title and Abstract Company or its assignee and Newbury News will assume the mortgage debt. Approximately two months later, the Alachua Alarmist, a weekly newspaper, will purchase the publishing plant from Williston Title and Abstract Company and Newbury News will deed the property to the Alachua Alarmist, which will pay the Williston Title and Abstract Company $105,000. Does this transaction qualify under § 1031? For whom?

CHAPTER 27

INVOLUNTARY CONVERSIONS AND OTHER DEFERRED RECOGNITION TRANSACTIONS

SECTION 1. INVOLUNTARY CONVERSIONS

1. Elton owns The Piano Men, a store that sells and repairs musical instruments. Elton runs the day-to-day operations of the business as his full-time job. Next to Elton's store, John owns Bubbles and Jets, a store that sells hot tubs. John has hired Diana to run the store and is not involved in the day-to-day operations. Elton and John each have an aggregate basis of $200,000 in their respective businesses. Unfortunately, when Elton came to work one morning, both buildings were ablaze and the buildings and everything inside was destroyed. Elton and John received $500,000 each from their insurance company.

   (a) What are the tax consequences of receiving the insurance settlement if Elton uses the money to purchase and operate a store that sells wigs and toupees?

   (b) What are the tax consequences of receiving the insurance settlement if John invests his $500,000 in a bookstore run by his friend Melissa?

2. (a) Billy owns an apartment building in which he has an adjusted basis of $250,000 and which is subject to a mortgage of $400,000. Recently, the city undertook to build a new baseball stadium in that area, and the building was taken by condemnation (eminent domain). Billy received $1,500,000, of which he used $400,000 to pay off the mortgage. A month later, Billy purchased another apartment building for $1,400,000. He paid $400,000 in cash and assumed an already existing mortgage of $1,000,000. If Billy decides to take advantage of § 1033, how much gain must he recognize? What will his basis in the new apartment building be?

   (b) How would your answer change if Billy had purchased a motel rather than the apartment building?

(c) How would your answer change in part 2(a) if the first apartment building burned to the ground (instead of being condemned), and Billy used $1,100,000 of the insurance proceeds to purchase a motel? The other $400,000 of insurance proceeds was used to pay of the mortgage on the apartment.

(d)(i) How would your answer to 2(a) change if Billy used the net $1,100,000 proceeds from the condemnation to purchase all the stock of a corporation whose sole asset was an apartment building?

(ii) What if Billy used the net proceeds to purchase 50 percent of the stock of a corporation that owned and operated an apartment building?

(iii) What if Billy, used the net $1,100,000, to purchase 100 percent of the stock of a corporation that owned and operated a motel?

3. Joel owns a coffee shop, Overpriced Caffeine Fix, which was located right next to Billy's old apartment building. It too was condemned to make way for the new stadium. Joel received $300,000 for the building that housed the coffee shop (it had an adjusted basis of $140,000). He sold all of the shop's equipment (cappuccino machines, tables, chairs, utensils, etc.), all of which had a basis of zero, for $70,000. He felt a bit burned out by his recent business activity, so he did not seek out any new ventures for a couple of years. Ultimately, in December of the third year after he received the condemnation award, he purchased a bookstore for $370,000 ($300,000 constituted the price of the building; the remainder covered books, furniture, etc.). To what extent may Joel claim nonrecognition under § 1033?

4. Del owned a computer store that that was totally destroyed by a tornado. Del received (1) $200,000 of insurance proceeds to cover the loss of the building, which had a basis of $120,000, (2) $160,000 of insurance proceeds to cover the loss of inventory, which had a basis of $70,000, and (3) $40,000 of insurance proceeds to cover his loss of equipment (registers, shelves, desks, etc.), in which he had an adjusted basis of zero. Del decided to try another business venture, a video rental store. He purchased a new building for $200,000, spent $70,000 for videos and DVDs in year 1 and $90,000 for videos and DVDs in year 2 and spent $40,000 for new equipment (registers, shelves, desks, etc. May Del use § 1033 to defer the gain he realized when he received the insurance proceeds?

PART VIII

TIMING OF INCOME AND DEDUCTIONS

CHAPTER 28

TAX ACCOUNTING METHODS

SECTION 2. THE CASH METHOD

1. Frieda leased Beryllium Acres (the site of a former mine) to Aqua Boy, who developed a children's water park on the site. Both Frieda and Aqua Boy are calendar year cash method taxpayers and are not related to one another. The rental agreement required annual rental payments of $30,000 due in advance on December 31 of the preceding year. In the following circumstances, when do Frieda and Aqua Boy account for the receipt and payment of the rental?

(a) Aqua Boy mailed the check on December 29. Frieda received the check on January 3.

(b) Aqua Boy wrote the check on December 31, but could not leave the annual Polar Bear swim and ice-skating event at the water park, so he could not mail it. Aqua Boy sent Frieda an e-mail notifying her that she could pick up the check if she desired. Frieda did not pick up the check and Aqua Boy put it in the mail on January 2. Frieda received the check on January 3.

(c) The lease was for five years. Frieda required a down payment of $100,000 at the time the lease was entered into, and annual payments of $30,000 due on December 31 of each year. How should Frieda and Aqua Boy treat the $100,000 payment made at the lease signing?

2. Peekaboo Powder is a professional ski instructor who works as an independent contractor at several ski areas. Peekaboo paid Razor Sharp $50 to tune three pairs of her skis. Peekaboo charged the ski tuning to her credit card on December 20. Razor Sharp submitted the charge receipt to the credit card company on December 27. Razor received payment from the credit card company on January 5. Peekaboo paid her credit card bill on January 15. Peekaboo and Razor are cash method calendar year taxpayers. When must Peekaboo and Razor account for their respective payment and income?

3. Peekaboo purchased various items of ski gear at Joan's Bike and Ski on December 22. She paid for the items using her Joan's Bike and Ski store credit account. Peekaboo paid this open account bill on January 15. Assuming that all of the purchased items are currently deductible, in which year may Peekaboo deduct the payments?

SECTION 3. THE ACCRUAL METHOD

A. INCOME ITEMS

1. (a) Joan's Bike and Ski leases space in a shopping center owned by Luke Landlord. Luke is an accrual method calendar year taxpayer. The lease calls for monthly rental payments of $1,500, due on the last day of each month. Joan paid the December rent by check delivered to Luke on January 2. In which year must Luke include the rent in income?

(b) The lease is a five-year lease that Luke and Joan executed on January 1. The lease agreement requires Joan to make a $2,000 nonrefundable payment on the same day, which Joan makes. In addition, the lease requires monthly rental payments of $1,500. When must Luke include the $2,000?

2. Hotwall-Bunker, Inc., a large real estate brokerage company, collects a 6 percent commission on every real estate transaction for which it acts as a broker. The commission is collected at the closing out of the proceeds due to the seller from the amount paid into escrow with the closing agent by the purchaser. However, it is customary to require purchasers to pay into an escrow amount as a deposit, an amount equal to 4 percent of the contracted sale and purchase price. The deposit is held in an escrow account by Hotwall-Bunker until the closing. If the purchaser defaults on the contract, Hotwall-Bunker is entitled to keep one-half of the deposit (equal to 2 percent of the contract price) and the seller gets the other one-half. If the sale and purchase closes, the closing agent sets off against the a 6 percent commission due to Hotwall-Bunker the deposit then being held by it and the closing agent disburses to Hotwall-Bunker an amount equal to an additional 2 percent of the purchase price (and Hotwall-Bunker transfers the entire deposit from its escrow account to its own account). As of December 31 of last year, Hotwall-Bunker was the broker with respect to $20,000,000 of pending real estate sales, with respect to which it held $800,000 in its escrow account. This year, all of the sales closed and Hotwall-Bunker transferred the $800,000 from its escrow account to its own account and received an additional $400,000 from the closing agents with respect to the sales. How much gross income is Hotwall-Bunker required to accrue in each year?

3. On January 1, the Eighteenth National Bank lent $1,000,000 to Divided Airlines Corp. at an annual interest rate of 8 percent. Interest was due and payable on December 31 each year. Divided Airlines filed for reorganization in bankruptcy on December 1. It is not clear whether the interest due to the Eighteenth National Bank will be paid when due, if ever. The Eighteenth National Bank is a calendar year accrual-method taxpayer. Must the Bank accrue the interest income due from Divided Airlines?

4. In January, Geraldo & Renaldo Truck Repair Inc. repaired a truck owned by Rich's Window Installation and submitted a bill for $1,200. The truck never ran right after the repair. Rich paid $300 of the bill for parts, but refused to pay the balance. By April, Rich decided that Geraldo & Renaldo would never be able to get the job done right and demanded a return of the $300 that he had already paid. Rich thereafter filed suit in small claims court for a return of the $300, which is still pending. Geraldo & Renaldo is a calendar year accrual-method taxpayer. Must Geraldo & Renaldo accrue any or all of the repair bill in the current year?

5. Aqua Boy Pools and Spas, Inc. sells a deluxe spa for $7,000. The price of the deluxe model includes two annual service visits for the first two years. Of the price of the deluxe model, $200 covers the service visits. Customers who purchase the standard model must pay $100 per service call, $25 of which is profit to Aqua Boy and $75 of which covers the cost of providing the service. Aqua Boy is a calendar year accrual-method taxpayer. When Aqua Boy sells a deluxe model, how should it account for the portion of the purchase price that is attributable to the service contract?

B. DEDUCTION ITEMS

1. (a) Benny's Bait Shop & Sushi Bar leases space in a shopping center owned by Lana. Benny is an accrual method calendar year taxpayer. The lease calls for monthly rental payments of $1,500, due on the last day of each month. Benny paid the December rent by check delivered to Lana on January 2. In which year can Benny deduct the rent?

(b) Does it make a difference in result if the rent is due in advance on the last day of the preceding month, but Benny actually paid the rent on January 2?

(c) The lease is a five-year lease that Lana and Benny executed on January 1. The lease agreement requires Benny to make a $2,000 nonrefundable payment on the same day, which Benny makes. In addition, the lease requires monthly rental payments of $1,500. When should Benny deduct the $2,000?

2. On January 1, the Eighteenth National Bank lent $1,000,000 to Outrun Energy Corp. ("OEC") at an annual interest rate of 8 percent. Interest was due and payable on December 31 each year. OEC filed for reorganization in bankruptcy on December 1. It is not clear whether the interest due to the Eighteenth National Bank will be paid when due, if ever. OEC is a calendar year accrual method taxpayer. May OEC accrue an interest deduction?

3. In January, Geraldo & Renaldo Truck Repair repaired a truck owned by Rich's Window Installation and submitted a bill for $2,500. The truck never ran right after the repair. Rich paid $300 of the bill for parts, but refused to pay the balance. By April, Rich decided that Geraldo & Renaldo would never be able to get the job done right and demanded a return of the $300 that he had already paid. Rich thereafter filed suit in small claims court for a return of the $800, which is still pending. Rich's Window Installation is a calendar year accrual method taxpayer. May Rich deduct any or all of the repair bill in the current year?

4. Aqua Boy Pools and Spas, Inc. sells a deluxe spa for $7,000. The price of the deluxe model includes two annual service visits for the first two years and $200 of the price of the deluxe model covers the service visits. Customers who purchase the standard model must pay $100 per service call, $25 of which is profit to Aqua Boy and $75 of which covers costs of providing the service. Aqua Boy is a calendar year accrual method taxpayer. When Aqua Boy sells a deluxe model, how should it account for the portion of the purchase price that is attributable to the $75 cost of providing service under the contract?

5. Paul Pickup was seriously injured in a rollover accident involving his Overpower Sports Utility Vehicle produced by Bad Design Motor Corp. Paul sued Bad Design and was awarded a $5,000,000 judgment. In a settlement agreement entered into to avoid appeal, Bad Design agreed to pay Paul $475,000 per year for 20 years. The present value of the payments is approximately $4,500,000 (using a 6 percent discount rate). Bad Design Motor Corp. is a calendar year accrual method taxpayer.

    (a) To what extent may Bad Design Motors deduct the settlement payments?

    (b) In the absence of § 461(h) what would be the after-tax cost of the settlement to Bad Design?

6. At its annual fall bicycle sale, Lance's Bike Shop gave each customer a lottery ticket for a December drawing for $1,000 in cash. The drawing was held on December 15 of the current year and publicized through a broadcast on the local cable television channel. The holder of the winning ticket did not present the ticket for redemption until January 15 of the following year, at which time Lance paid the cash prize. Lance's Bike Shop is a calendar year accrual method taxpayer. In which year may Lance deduct the prize?

7. Polonius is in the business of making plastic skulls and uses the accrual method of accounting. He occasionally retains his son Laertes, a lawyer, to perform routine legal services. Laertes uses the cash method of accounting. On December 15, Polonius received a bill from Laertes for services rendered during the month of November. The bill states that it is due and payable by December 31. The end-of-year rush makes Polonius fall behind on his paperwork and he does not get around to writing the check to Laertes until January 2 of the following year. When can Polonius deduct the payment of Laertes's bill? When must Laertes include the amount in income?

SECTION 4. INVENTORY ACCOUNTING

1. Benny Jett manages the computer network at the University of Gotham City Law School. Benny is a cash method calendar year taxpayer. In his spare time, Benny reconditions and upgrades old computers for resale. In the current year, Benny purchased 20 used computers and monitors for $150 each. Benny spends another $300 per computer for upgraded memory chips, hard drives, and a new processing chip. Thus, Benny's total cost was $9,000. Benny sold 15 reconditioned machines during the year for $1,500 each, resulting in total gross receipts of $22,500.

   (a) How should Benny report his receipts and expenditures for the year?

   (b) How does your answer change if Benny purchased five of the computers for $75 each in February, ten computers for $100 each in July, and five computers for $125 each in October, assuming that Benny continues to spend $300 per computer for the upgrades?

   (c) If Benny behaves as described in (b) above, should he adopt the first-in, first-out (FIFO) method or the last-in, first-out (LIFO) method?

2. Explain why major oil companies would like to adopt LIFO inventory methods in periods of rising oil prices. Should the oil companies that use LIFO for tax purposes be permitted to report their financial results on the FIFO method?

CHAPTER 29

THE ANNUAL ACCOUNTING CONCEPT

SECTION 1. TRANSACTIONAL PROBLEMS

B. INITIAL DEDUCTION FOLLOWED BY LATER RECOVERY: THE TAX BENEFIT DOCTRINE

1. (a) Last year, BillyJo's Worm Farm & Apple Orchard, Inc. paid $8,000 in county real estate taxes, which it properly deducted. This year, pursuant to an appeal of the prior year's real estate tax assessment, BillyJo's Worm Farm will receive a tax rebate of $3,000 from the county. How much, if any, of the $3,000 must, BillyJo's Worm Farm include in gross income?

   (b) Would your answer differ if the amount paid last year was an assessment for sewer improvements by the county?

   (c) What would the consequences be if the real estate taxes had been paid with respect to BillyJo's personal residence and the $8,000 of real estate taxes was BillyJo's only itemized deduction (assuming that if BillyJo had not itemized deductions her standard deduction would have been $6,000)?

2. Two years ago Joan's Bike and Ski Shop hired Eldon to paint murals of a skier and a mountain biker on the exterior walls of the shop. When Eldon completed the work, Joan's Bike and Ski gave him a check for $5,000 dated October 31, which bore the legend "void if not cashed within 90 days." Joan's Bike and Ski Shop properly deducted the $5,000 as a business expense under § 162. Eldon has never cashed the check despite the lapse of over a year, and the bank will no longer honor the check. Eldon's telephone has been disconnected, and he is no longer listed in the city directory or with the Chamber of Commerce. Is Joan's Bike and Ski Shop required to include the previously deducted $5,000 in gross income?

C. INITIAL INCLUSION IN INCOME FOLLOWED BY LATER REPAYMENT

1. Beginning in Year 1, the Gulf Coast Oil Co. and the United States government were engaged in a legal dispute over the title to a certain oil field. As a result, the Government appointed a receiver for the property, and all of the income earned in Year 1 from the property was paid to the receiver, rather than to Gulf Coast. In Year 2, a district court determined that Gulf Coast had title to the property, and therefore ordered the receiver to return all of the Year 1 income to Gulf Coast. Under the claim of right doctrine (discussed in Chapter 5), Gulf Coast therefore included these earnings in income in Year 2. Suppose that the district court's decision was reversed on appeal in Year 8, at which time Gulf Coast was ordered to repay the Year 1 earnings to the government. Assume that this repayment would qualify as a deductible business expense under § 162 and that the Year 1 earnings amounted to $1,000,000. What are the Year 8 income tax consequences to Gulf Coast from the repayment under the following circumstances?

   (a) The marginal tax rate applicable to Gulf Coast in Year 2 was 20 percent, while its Year 8 marginal tax rate was 35 percent.

   (b) The marginal tax rate applicable to Gulf Coast in Year 2 was 35 percent, while its Year 8 marginal tax rate was 20 percent.

SECTION 2. NET OPERATING LOSS CARRYOVER AND CARRYBACK

1. Bubba's Bait & Tackle, Inc. has had a varied earnings history over the past twelve years because of the impact of weather on the fishing season and demand for new equipment. Before accounting for loss carryforwards and carrybacks, Bubba's Bait & Tackle's taxable income has been as follows:

Year	Income (Loss)
1	($ 5,000)
2	$10,000
3	$20,000
4	$ 0
5	($ 6,000)
6	$10,000
7	($50,000)
8	$30,000
9	$60,000
10	$50,000
11	($10,000)
12	$30,000

Assuming that current law is applicable to all of these years, what is Bubba's Bait & Tackle's taxable income in each year after taking into account loss carryforward and carryback provisions?

CHAPTER 30

DEFERRED COMPENSATION ARRANGEMENTS

SECTION 1. NONQUALIFIED DEFERRED COMPENSATION CONTRACTS

1. In Year 5, Joe Idaho, an All-American quarterback at Sisters of Mercy University, signed a 10-year contract to play professional football for the Reno Raiders. His complex compensation package is as follows. Upon signing, Joe received $500,000 in cash. In addition, the Raiders promised to pay Joe an additional $1 million in cash when he reported to training camp in Year 6. The $1 million payment would be paid on July 1, Year 6. If Joe made the team after training camp (a virtual certainty), the Raiders would pay Joe a bonus of $1.5 million on September 1, Year 6, and he would also receive a salary of $2 million for Year 6 and each of the next nine years, even if he did not play for the team in any succeeding year. If the team gets to the Super Bowl, Joe will be entitled to an additional $1 million in that year. Joe went to training camp and made the team. When must Joe include the various payments in his income, and when may the Raiders claim deductions for the payments? The team has not yet made it to the Super Bowl since signing Joe.

2. Kenny's compensation agreement with Charged Energy Corporation ("CEC") entitles him to an annual salary of $150,000; in addition, CEC must either pay Kenny additional supplemental compensation of $200,000 or deposit that amount into an escrow account with the Eighteenth National Bank to fund an annuity that will enable Kenny to receive payments when he retires. Before January 1 of each year Kenny must tell CEC how he wants the following year's supplemental compensation paid: check made out to him or escrow deposit. Kenny is a cash method, calendar year taxpayer.

   (a) Must Kenny include in his income supplemental compensation that is deposited in the Eighteenth National Bank?

   (b) Must Kenny include interest paid on the amount of supplemental compensation accumulated in the Eighteenth National Bank account?

   (c) Can Kenny's contract be re-written to defer taxation? How?

(d) What are the advantages and disadvantages of deferred taxation to Kenny?

(e) Under either arrangement, when is CEC entitled to deduct Kenny's supplemental compensation?

SECTION 2. TRANSFERS OF PROPERTY FOR SERVICES

1. Hank Hurler was drafted by the San Juan Expos as the number 1 draft pick in the major league baseball draft last year. As part of his signing bonus, the Expos paid Imprudent Insurance Co. $500,000 for a single premium annuity policy that would pay Hank $100,000 a year for the next 10 years. In addition the Expos promised to purchase a second identical annuity policy if and when Hank made the major leagues. After spending last year playing in the minor leagues with the St. Petersburg Bay Manta Rays, this year Hank made the big leagues and the Expos purchased the second annuity contract. How much gross income must Hank recognize? When?

2. (a) Leon, who previously worked for Lo Tech Corp., recently moved to Cherry Computer Corp., a new, innovative computer hardware company. To induce Leon to join Cherry Computer, the corporation offered him, in addition to his salary, the opportunity to purchase 1,000 shares of common stock at $10 a share, and an option to purchase an additional 1,000 shares each year for the next five years at $20 per share. Cherry Computer stock is not publicly traded, but several investors recently paid $20 per share in private placements. The 1,000 shares Leon purchased when he joined Cherry Computer must be resold to Cherry Computer at $10 per share if Leon leaves the corporation any time within three years of the purchase. Thereafter, the shares need not be resold to Cherry Computer unless Leon goes to work for a competitor within 10 years of the date of purchase, in which case they must still be resold at $10 per share. Leon may transfer stock purchased pursuant to the options, but stock owned by a transferee is subject to the same restrictions to which it would be subject if owned by Leon. The options are not transferable and are exercisable only as long as Leon is an employee. Any stock purchased pursuant to the options will be subject to the same restrictions as the original stock. What are the income tax consequences of this arrangement for Leon and for Cherry Computer?

(b) What factors should be considered in advising Leon whether or not to make an election under § 83(b) upon purchase of the stock?

(c) What would be the amount and character of Leon's gain with respect to the original 1,000 shares if he made a § 83(b) election and sold the stock 11 years later for $110 per share?

3. (a) Javier is a vice-president of Pan American Airlines, a publicly held corporation traded on the New York Stock Exchange. In June of last year, Javier was granted, as a bonus, an option to purchase 5,000 shares of stock in Pan American for $10 per share. At the time the option was granted, Pan American was trading at $10 per share. Similar options to buy Pan American at $10 pcr share had recently sold privately for $2, but such options were not traded on an established market. Javier's option was, by its express terms, nontransferable. This November, Javier exercised his option when Pan American was selling for $40 a share. One week later, he sold for $50 per share 1,000 shares of the Pan American stock that he had just purchased. What are the tax consequences of these events for Javier?

(b) Would your answer to part (a) be different if Pan American options were actively traded on an established securities market?

4. (a) How would your answer in Problem 3(a) be different if Javier's option was an incentive stock option under § 422, and the Pan American stock was trading at $8 per share on the day the option was granted?

(b) What would be the amount and character of Javier's gain if in December of the year following the year in which he exercised the options he sold for $50 per share 1,000 of the Pan American shares purchased pursuant to the incentive stock option?

(c) What would be the amount and character of Javier's gain if he received the incentive stock option in June of the year before last (year 1), exercised the option in February of last year (year 2), and sold 1,000 of the Pan American shares for $50 per share in March of this year (year 3)?

CHAPTER 31

DEFERRED PAYMENT SALES

SECTION 1. NONSTATUTORY DEFERRED REPORTING OF GAINS

1. Would you advise the Internal Revenue Service to adopt the approach of either *Burnet v. Logan* or *Warren Jones Co. v. Commissioner* or should it retain Treasury Regulation § 1.1001-1(g)?

SECTION 2. INSTALLMENT REPORTING UNDER SECTION 453

1. Bonaparte Corp. sold unimproved land held for investment to Lewis Clark for $500,000. Lewis paid $50,000 in cash and gave Bonaparte Corp. a promissory note, secured by the land, for $450,000, payable over 5 years, in annual installments of $90,000 of principal plus all accrued interest. The note bore adequate stated interest. Bonaparte Corp.'s basis in the land was $200,000.

   (a) Assuming that Bonaparte Corp. does not make a § 453(d) election, what are the tax consequences of this transaction to Bonaparte Corp. in the year of sale and in each year Bonaparte Corp. receives a payment on the note?

   (b) What are the tax consequences of the sale if Bonaparte Corp. makes a § 453(d) election?

2. LeBron owns undeveloped land in Cleveland worth $300,000. It has a basis of $120,000 and is subject to a $60,000 mortgage. LeBron sells the property to Carmelo, who assumes the mortgage, pays LeBron $60,000 cash, and gives him a note for $180,000, to be paid in three annual installments with interest at a market rate.

   (a) What are the tax consequences to LeBron in the year of the sale?

   (b) What are the tax consequences to LeBron when he receives annual payments in the years after the sale?

(c) What if the mortgage was $150,000 and Carmelo purchased the property by assuming the mortgage and signing a note for $150,000 payable in three annual installments of $50,000 (bearing interest at a market rate)?

3. Michael owned 100 percent of the shares of Just Do It, a closely held corporation that sells sports apparel. In January of this year, Michael sold 100 shares in Just Do It to his son, Julius, for $20,000 in cash plus Julius' note for $80,000 (with market interest) payable in eight annual installments. Michael's basis in the stock was $20,000.

(a) What are the tax consequences to Michael and Julius if, before making any payments on the note, Julius sells the stock to his friend, Larry, for $80,000?

(b) What are the tax consequences to Michael and Julius if Julius sells the stock to Larry for $70,000?

(c) What if Julius sells the stock to Larry for $110,000?

(d) What if Julius makes a $10,000 payment of principal on the note and then sells the stock to Larry for $100,000?

4. In September, Darla Disposition sold a parcel of undeveloped land to Earl Enstallment for $200,000. Earl purchased the land by giving Darla a $200,000 promissory note, secured by the property, with stated annual interest of 6 percent payable in five years. Darla's basis in the land was $20,000 and she has held the land for more than one year.

(a) In June of the current year, Darla sold the note to the Third National Bank for $180,000. What is the tax consequence of the sale of the note?

(b) Instead of selling the note, when the fair market value of the obligation is $180,000, Darla gives the note to her daughter Mal. Mal holds the note to maturity and collects the principal and interest. What are the tax consequences to Mal Disposition when she collects the note?

(c) What is the consequence if Darla dies one year after the sale and bequeaths the note to her daughter Mal who collects the principal and interest at maturity?

5. Gail Grease owned 100 percent of the stock of Grease Corp. Gail's basis in the Grease Corp. stock was $30,000. Grease Corp.'s sole asset was a patent on a voice-activated point-of-sale ordering system for fast food restaurants and a contract with Chuck's In-and-Up BBQ chain for installation of the system. Gail sold her Grease Corp. stock to the Burrow Business Systems Corp. for

$10,000 cash plus five percent of the gross sales of the point-of-sale system for the next fifteen years. Assume that the payments work out to be $10,000 in each of the first six years and $15,000 in each of the next nine years.

(a)How should Gail report the transaction in the year of sale and in the subsequent years if she does not file an election under § 453(d)?

(b) What if Gail files the § 453(d) election?

CHAPTER 32

INTEREST ON DISCOUNT OBLIGATIONS

SECTION 2. ORIGINAL ISSUE DISCOUNT

1. Dixie Chicken Corp. is planning to issue bonds to raise cash to expand its business operations. Consider the following transactions.

(a) On June 30 of the current year Dixie Chicken Corp. issues bonds with a face value of $1,000,000, due in 10 years, which pay zero stated interest, for an issue price of $376,889.50.

> (i) How much interest may Dixie Chicken Corp. deduct during the current year and the next year?

> (ii) EmmyLou purchased $100,000 face value of Dixie Chicken Corp.'s bonds for $37,688.95. How much interest must EmmyLou include during current the year and the next year?

(b) On June 30, Dixie Chicken Corp. issues for face value $1,000,000, ten-year bonds that bear interest at the prime rate plus 1 percent, which you may assume for all relevant periods computes to 6 percent. Interest is payable semi-annually. The applicable federal rate for the current year is 7 percent.

> (i) How much interest may Dixie Chicken Corp. deduct in the current year?

> (ii) Dolly purchased $100,000 face value of Dixie Chicken Corp.'s bonds for $100,000. How much interest must Dolly include during the current year and the next year?

(c) On June 30, Dixie Chicken Corp. issues for face value $1,000,000 of ten-year bonds bearing interest at 10 percent, payable semi-annually, but no interest is due and payable until the second anniversary of the bond issue. The applicable federal rate is 7 percent. How do you determine whether the bonds are OID instruments?

(d) Dixie Chicken Corp. issues $1,000,000 of ten-year convertible bonds. Each bond is convertible into Dixie Chicken Corp. common stock at any time prior to redemption at an exchange ratio of one share of stock for $10 of bonds. When the bonds were issued, Dixie Chicken Corp. stock was trading on the stock exchange at $9.50 per share. The bonds pay interest annually at 7 percent. The applicable federal rate was 7 percent when the bonds were issued. Are the bonds OID bonds?

2. Osprey Realty Development Corp. purchased the California Hotel from Glenn. In exchange for the California, Glenn received an Osprey bond in the face amount of $10,000,000 due in ten years. No express interest is due on the bond. At the time of the sale, the applicable federal rate was 7 percent.

(a) What is Osprey's basis for the California Hotel? If the deal closed on June 30, how much interest may Osprey deduct in the year of the sale? How much interest must Glenn include in the year of the sale?

(b) Suppose that the stated principal amount of the bond was $5,000,000 and interest accrued at 7 percent compounded semi-annually, but no interest was payable until the bond was due in 10 years. At that time, Glenn was to receive the $5,000,000 principal and $4,948,944 interest, for a total amount due of $9,948,944. How much interest must Glenn include in income and how much interest may Osprey deduct for the year of sale?

3. Bruce sold his vacation condominium on Maui to Nora for $240,000. At the closing on July 1, Nora paid Bruce $40,000 in cash and gave him a promissory note, secured by a mortgage, for $200,000. The note provided for no interest. The note was payable in installments of $20,000, due on July 1 of each of the next ten years. Bruce's basis in his condominium was $80,000. The applicable federal rate on the closing date was 5 percent. What is the amount realized on the sale by Bruce? How much interest income does Bruce recognize? When? What is Nora's basis in the property? How much interest has she paid? When did she pay it?

4. (a) On December 31, Year 26, Sheryl paid $18,000 to purchase on the market a debenture bond issued in Year 13 by Rock Industries, Inc. The bond had an issue price of $20,000, paid 8 percent interest per year and $20,000 upon maturity, and was due on December 31, Year 28. What will be the character of Sheryl's gain upon redemption of the bond?

(b) What would be the character of Sheryl's gain if she sold the bond for $19,800 on September 30, Year 28, three months before redemption?

SECTION 3. BOND PREMIUM

1. On July 1, Year 1, Adam Smith purchased a newly issued $100,000 debenture issued by the Pari-Mutuel Insurance Company, Inc. The stated terms of the bond provided for annual interest at 10 percent, payable semiannually with the principal due on July 1, Year 10. Because interest rates had fallen between the time the bonds and the prospectus were printed, to adjust for the higher than market stated interest rate, the bonds were sold for $102,500.

(a) What are the tax consequences to Adam when he receives $5,000 of interest in Year 1? When he receives $10,000 of interest in Year 2? When he receives the $100,000 principal payment in Year 10?

(b) What are the tax consequences to Pari-Mutuel Insurance Co.?

PART IX

TAX MOTIVATED TRANSACTIONS

CHAPTER 33

TRANSACTIONS INVOLVING LEASED PROPERTY

1. In Estate of *Starr*, the court suggests that after the Commissioner "has made allowance for depreciation, which he concedes, and an allowance for interest, the attack on many of the "leases" may not be worthwhile in terms of revenue." Is the court correct in its observation? Why or why not?

2. (a) OrganDonor Motorcycle Mfg. Co. leased an office building for its corporate headquarters from ServiceCard Credit Corporation. The twenty-five-year lease required OrganDonor to pay a monthly rent of $50,000 ($600,000 per year). Concurrently with the execution of the lease, ServiceCard gave OrganDonor an option to purchase the building at any time during the term of the lease. The purchase price under the option was $10,000,000 in the

first year, but increased by $500,000 in each subsequent year. If OrganDonor exercised the option, 50 percent of its previously paid rent (i.e., $300,000 per year) would be credited against the purchase price. Is this a true lease by ServiceCard to OrganDonor, or is it an installment sale? What difference does it make to each?

(b) Would your answer differ if 80 percent of the rent would be credited against the purchase price?

(c) Would your answer to part (b) differ if the purchase price increased by only $100,000 per year?

(d) Would your answer to part (a) (50 percent of the cumulative rent paid by OrganDonor would be credited against the purchase price) differ if the purchase price increased by only $100,000 per year?

3. (a) WallyWorld Inc. is a corporation that operates a number of theme parks on over 20,000 acres of land in Nevada. WallyWorld has not been in operation very long and has not yet generated a profit. Although WallyWorld does not expect to generate a profit for either tax or financial accounting purposes for several years, it continues to need substantial amounts of cash to remain in business. To obtain cash on better terms than it could receive from a bank, WallyWorld recently agreed to sell to Cashcow Inc. all of the light rail passenger cars used to operate the WallyWorld inter-park transportation system. Cashcow agreed to pay $20 million for the cars, the amount an independent appraiser opined was the fair market value of the cars. Under the terms of the agreement, Cashcow agreed to pay WallyWorld the $20 million upon receipt of title to the cars at closing, and WallyWorld agreed to lease the cars for a period of 10 years, for an annual rental of $2.2 million. The lease is to be a net lease whereby WallyWorld is to pay all maintenance, repair, and operational costs attributable to the cars, including any use, occupancy or other excise taxes, and is required to insure them under terms that would allow Cashcow to receive the insurance proceeds if the cars were in any way lost or damaged. The lease is silent regarding renewals or transfer of title at the end of the lease term. Will Cashcow be entitled to take deductions for depreciation on the cars it bought from and leased to WallyWorld? Why or why not?

(b) Does your answer change if WallyWorld is required to obtain a letter of credit that will ensure the payment of its obligations under the lease?

(c) Does your answer change if it is reasonably estimated that the cars will have only negligible salvage value at the end of the lease term?

(d) Does your answer change if WallyWorld has an option to purchase the cars at the end of the lease term for an amount equal to 20 percent of the amount determined by an independent appraiser to be the fair market value of the cars at that time? What if the option price is 80 percent of the appraised value?

(e) Does your answer change if instead of buying railroads cars from WallyWorld, Cashcow buys WallyWorld's fleet of maintenance trucks and corporate passenger vehicles, the lease term is only five years, and there is no purchase option?

CHAPTER 34

NONRECOURSE DEBT AND LEVERAGED TAX SHELTERS

SECTION 1. ACQUISITION AND DISPOSITION OF PROPERTY SUBJECT TO NONRECOURSE DEBT

1. Donald purchased a parcel of undeveloped land in College Town for $100,000. Subsequently, Donald constructed an apartment complex on the land at a cost of $900,000. The construction was financed with a $900,000 nonrecourse loan from the Eighth Bank of College Town, secured by a mortgage on the property. Donald operated the property for rental income over seven years. During that period Donald claimed $230,000 of depreciation deductions with respect to the building, and made principal payments on the outstanding indebtedness in the amount of $50,000, plus interest.

(a)(i) At the end of the seven year period, Donald sold the land and building to Leona, who took the property subject to the mortgage, which she did not expressly assume, and gave Donald a check for $350,000. What is Donald's amount realized and his recognized gain or loss?

(ii) What is Leona's basis?

(b) Suppose alternatively that after the end of Donald's seven year operation of the apartment complex, its fair market value had declined to $700,000, and Donald transferred the complex to Leona, who paid him no cash but simply took the property subject to the outstanding mortgage, again without expressly assuming the liability. What is Donald's amount realized and his recognized gain or loss?

(c)(i) Would your answer to part (b) differ if instead of Donald transferring the apartment complex to Leona, the Eighth Bank of College Town foreclosed on the mortgage?

(ii) Would your answer to part (c)(1) differ if in lieu of foreclosure, Donald transferred the apartment complex to the Eighth Bank of College Town by quitclaim deed?

2. Cliff purchased Blackacre for $80,000 in cash, taking the property subject to an outstanding $70,000 nonrecourse mortgage debt. Subsequently, Cliff borrowed $75,000 on a nonrecourse basis from the Debby Finance Company, giving Debby Finance a second mortgage on Blackacre. Cliff used $30,000 of the second mortgage loan proceeds to install a drainage system on Blackacre. He used $45,000 of the loan proceeds to acquire a new automobile. A few years later when the outstanding balance of the first mortgage loan was $55,000 and the outstanding balance of the second mortgage was $65,000, Cliff transferred Blackacre to Joe, who took the property subject to the outstanding first and second mortgages and gave a check to Cliff in the amount of $80,000. What is Cliff's amount realized on the disposition of Blackacre? How much gain or loss must Cliff recognize?

3. Ellen purchased Whiteacre for $100,000 in cash. Subsequently, when Whiteacre had appreciated in value to $500,000, Ellen borrowed $300,000 on a nonrecourse basis from the Harsha Finance Company, giving Harsha Finance a second mortgage on Whiteacre. Ellen used $300,000 to purchase New York Stock Exchange traded stock. A few years later when the outstanding balance of the mortgage loan was still $300,000 and the fair market value of Whiteacre was only $250,000, Ellen deeded the property to Harsha Finance in lieu of foreclosure. How much gain or loss must Ellen recognize?

4. (a) Charlotte purchased a residential rental property for $500,000. She financed the purchase with a $450,000 interest only nonrecourse mortgage loan with a balloon payment due at the end of ten years. Five years later when the basis of the property was $440,000 (after deducting $60,000 of depreciation), Charlotte transferred the property to her daughter Janet as a gift. The fair market value of the property on the date of the gift was $550,000. Does Charlotte recognize gain or loss as a result of the transfer?

(b) What if the property were transferred to Janet on account of Charlotte's death?

(c) What if at the time of Charlotte's death the fair market value of the property had declined to $400,000?

SECTION 3. THE VALUATION OF PROPERTY SUBJECT TO DEBT

1. Donald owned an apartment complex in College Town, the acquisition of which was financed with a nonrecourse mortgage loan from the Eighth Bank of College Town. At a time when the value of the property was only $700,000,

Donald transferred the building to Leona, who took the property subject to the outstanding nonrecourse mortgage, the outstanding balance on which was $850,000. What is Leona's basis?

2. Brown's Parcel Service wanted to offset some of the substantial income generated by its business. Brown struck a deal with Anson's Fine Equipment Corp. whereby Brown would purchase Anson's manufacturing plant for $21,000,000 with a seller-financed nonrecourse mortgage of $20,000,000, and an initial cash payment of $1,000,000. Other than the initial cash payment, the mortgage agreement provided for no payment of principal until 15 years from the date of purchase, at which point the amount outstanding on the loan would be due all at once in a balloon payment. In addition, Brown agreed to lease the property back to Anson's Fine Equipment Corp. for a monthly rental payment that exactly offset the monthly interest due on the nonrecourse mortgage. Brown immediately began taking large depreciation deductions, using an initial basis of $21,000,000 for the property. The IRS suspects that the rental property was actually worth no more than $800,000 when Brown purchased it. Under what two judicially developed theories might Brown's depreciation deductions be disallowed?

CHAPTER 35

STATUTORY LIMITATIONS ON LEVERAGED TAX SHELTERS

SECTION 1. THE AT-RISK LIMITATION

1. (a) Calvin invested $20,000 to become a one-tenth partner in a partnership formed to purchase a commuter airliner for lease to PanWorld Airlines. The partnership purchased the airliner for $2,000,000 by paying $200,000 down and borrowing $1,800,000 from the Last National Savings and Loan Association on a nonrecourse basis, with the loan secured by the airliner. Calvin's basis in his partnership interest, including his share of the note, is $200,000. In the first year, interest, depreciation, and expenses exceeded rental income from the airliner by $500,000. To what extent may Calvin deduct his one-tenth share, $50,000, of the net partnership loss?

(b) In the second year of operation, the airliner produced rental income of $100,000 in excess of deductible expense items. What is the tax consequence to Calvin of his $10,000 partnership share of net income?

(c) What would be the difference in parts (a) and (b) if the partners had personally guaranteed the purchase-money promissory note?

(d) Would your answer to part (a) differ if Calvin had borrowed his $20,000 share of the initial $200,000 investment from Joseph, another partner in the partnership?

2. (a) In Problem 1(a), what would be the result if, instead of purchasing an airplane, the partnership had purchased an apartment building with the nonrecourse loan, secured by the apartment building?

(b) Would your answer differ if instead of borrowing the purchase price from the bank, the partnership gave a nonrecourse note to the seller from whom it purchased the property?

SECTION 2. PASSIVE ACTIVITY LOSS LIMITATION

1. (a) J.P., a wealthy investment banker, purchased an office building for $2 million, borrowing the entire purchase price from the Last Texas Savings and Loan. The loan is nonrecourse, secured by the land and building, and constitutes "qualified nonrecourse financing" under § 465(b)(6). (In other words, J.P. is considered to be at risk for the full amount of the loan, so the at-risk limitation of § 465 does not apply). Principal and interest on the note are payable over 20 years. J.P did not invest any of her own money and did not devote any of her time to managing the office building.

   In the first year of operations, the results for J.P. are as follows:

Rental income	$270,000
Interest paid	$210,000
Operating expenses	$ 50,000
Depreciation	$ 60,000

   Although J.P. properly claimed $60,000 of depreciation deductions on the building for the year, its fair market value actually declined by only $20,000. In addition to the interest payment, J.P. made a $20,000 principal payment on the note. J.P. has $800,000 of salary income from her investment banking job and $80,000 of dividend income from portfolio investments. To what extent may J.P. deduct her net $50,000 loss from the office building?

   (b) On the first day of the second year, J.P. sold the building. Since the value of the building exactly equaled the $1,980,000 mortgage on the building, the buyer simply took the building subject to the mortgage, and J.P. received no other consideration. What are the tax consequences of the sale to J.P.?

   (c) Assume that instead of selling the building, in the second year J.P. receives $320,000 of rental income net of all expenses except for interest and depreciation. J.P. pays $200,000 of interest on the loan, and depreciation is again $60,000. J.P.'s salary and dividend income are the same as in the first year. What are the tax consequences of J.P.'s investment in the office building in year two?

   (d) In part (a), what would be the tax consequence in year one if J.P. also owned a second rental property that produced $40,000 of income net of all expenses, including interest and depreciation?

2. Jerry and Kathy each contributed $1,000,000 and together purchased a small office building for $2,000,000. For the current year they realized an operating loss of $40,000 — $20,000 each. Jerry is engaged primarily in the construction

business, from which his annual income is $250,000; Kathy is a physician and earns $300,000 annually.

(a) Jerry serves as leasing agent and manages the building. Kathy performs no services for the partnership. May either Jerry or Kathy deduct his or her share of the operating losses against his or her other income?

(b) Kathy serves as leasing agent and manages the building. Jerry performs no services for the partnership. May either Jerry or Kathy deduct his or her share of partnership losses against his or her other income?

3. Bernie is involved in two related business undertakings, a video arcade in Daytona Beach and a video arcade in Jacksonville. In each of the following circumstances, would Bernie be better off treating the two undertakings as one activity or as two?

(a) Bernie materially participates in the Daytona Beach video arcade, but not in the Jacksonville video arcade. During the current year, the Daytona Beach video arcade generates a loss of $100,000, and the Jacksonville video arcade generates a loss of $150,000. Bernie has a salary of $300,000. There are no other relevant facts.

(b) Bernie materially participates in the Daytona Beach video arcade, but not in the Jacksonville video arcade. During the current year, the Daytona Beach video arcade produces income of $100,000, and the Jacksonville video arcade produces income of $150,000. Bernie also has a $120,000 loss from an apartment building in Philadelphia, which is clearly an activity separate from both the Daytona Beach video arcade and the Jacksonville video arcade. There are no other relevant facts.

(c) Bernie does not materially participate in either undertaking. There are substantial § 469(b) passive loss carryforwards with respect to each undertaking. Bernie sells his entire interest in the Daytona Beach video arcade, but retains his interest in the Jacksonville video arcade.

4. David is a college professor who earned a salary of $120,000 last year. He owns two strip malls, Parkwood and Timber Village. During last year, Parkwood generated a loss of $80,000, and Timber Village produced income of $50,000. The two buildings constituted separate activities. David also had $20,000 income last year from a pecan farm that was a non-real estate passive activity. To what extent may David deduct the loss from Parkwood?

5. Jane is an actress who is a 10 percent partner in the Macon Braves, a minor league baseball team. The Macon Braves partnership had a net loss in the

current year. Jane's basis in her partnership interest, prior to taking into account this year's loss, is $150,000.

(a) Jane is a limited partner. She performed no services for the Macon Braves. Her distributive share from the Macon Braves was a $60,000 loss. She earned $2,000,000 from acting this year. May she deduct her distributive share of Macon Braves' losses against her acting income?

(b) What would be your answer to (a) if Jane were instead a general partner?

(c) Assume that Jane is a general partner. She took a hiatus from her acting career and served as the team's general manager, for which she received a guaranteed payment of $40,000. Her distributive share from the Macon Braves was a $60,000 loss. She received $200,000 of interest and dividends on publicly traded securities this year. May she deduct her distributive share of Macon Braves losses against her income from serving as the manager and her interest and dividend income?

(d) Assume that Jane is a general partner, but the only service she performed for the partnership was to "star" in three filmed television commercials, for which she received $10,000. Her distributive share from the Macon Braves was a $60,000 loss. She earned $1,000,000 from acting this year. May she deduct her distributive share of Macon Braves losses against her income from the commercial and her other acting income?

(e) Jane is a limited partner. She performed no services for the Macon Braves. Her distributive share from the Macon Braves was a $60,000 loss; that loss consisted of $5,000 of interest income on the working capital of the Macon Braves and a $65,000 loss from other items. Jane earned $2,000,000 from acting this year. What portion of the $65,000 loss will Jane be able to deduct his year?

(f) What would be the result in (a), above, if Jane also realized $45,000 of net income from a real estate limited partnership interest, in which she has invested as a limited partner?

CHAPTER 36

ECONOMIC SUBSTANCE DOCTRINE

1. The Contingent Deferred Swap transaction, which was marketed by a well-known accounting firm, involves an investment in a notional principal contract that calls for a periodic payment by the investor's partnership based on London Interbank Offer Rate (LIBOR) applied to a notional amount, and an offsetting payment form a counter-party based on a fixed interest rate applied to 92 percent of the notional amount and a fluctuating index such as the S&P 500 applied to 8 percent of the notional amount. Marketing materials provided to investors illustrated the transaction as producing a $20 million ordinary loss deduction in year one that is offset with $20 million of capital gain in year two. The actual investment depended on the amount of loss the investor desires to generate in the first year. The actual economic result of the transaction will vary with the fluctuation of LIBOR and the S&P 500, although the amount of the economic gain or loss is restricted by collars and caps. Some investors suffered economic loss, some achieved an economic gain. Regardless of the economic return, the transaction produces a large after-tax return because the first-year losses offset substantial income (often derived from the exercise of stock options). The first-year loss is converted into capital gain in the second year.

   Assume that the claimed benefits of the transaction are otherwise available under a literal application of the relevant provisions of the Code and Regulations. Do you think this transaction would survive scrutiny under the economic substance/business purpose doctrine?

2. Do you think *Compaq* would have been decided differently or more easily if § 7701(o) had been effective at the time the parties entered into the transaction? Do you think that the taxpayers would have entered into the transactions at issue in those cases?

PART X

THE TAXABLE UNIT

C H A P T E R 37

SHIFTING INCOME AMONG TAXABLE UNITS

SECTION 1. INCOME FROM PERSONAL SERVICES

1. (a) Tammy is employed as a research manager for BioTech, Inc. for an annual salary of $130,000. BioTech maintains a written plan that provides for payment of up to $10,000 per year of college education expenses for the children of employees. Tammy's daughter Anne is enrolled in Elite University and BioTech directly paid $10,000 of Anne's tuition to the University. Who is taxable on the tuition payment?

    (b)(i) After Anne graduated, Tammy was so pleased with Anne's education that Tammy pledged $24,000 of her next year's earnings to Elite University. Tammy made a written assignment of the income that the University delivered to BioTech, Inc. In the following year, BioTech paid the $24,000 directly to Elite University. Will Tammy recognize income with respect to the $24,000 BioTech paid to Elite University?

(ii) Does the answer change if instead of directing the income to Elite University, Tammy asked the board of directors of BioTech to reduce her salary by $24,000 and to pay $2,000 per month to any worthwhile charity that the board of directors should select? What if the board selects Elite University?

2. (a) Duffy Dungeness is a 60-year-old attorney who has built up a relatively small, but highly successful, law practice in Monterey, California. Duffy's daughter and only child, Eunice, just graduated in the top of her class from Big University Law School. Eunice was heavily recruited by New York law firms at salaries that ranged from $100,000 to $150,000. Nevertheless, Eunice decided to join her father's law practice as an employee. Duffy agreed to pay her a yearly salary of $50,000 as well as a bonus equal to half of the practice's profits in excess of $50,000. During their first year of practice together Duffy and Eunice earned $550,000 of net income, after payment of Eunice's $50,000 salary. Duffy then distributed $50,000 to himself, and Duffy and Eunice divided the remaining $500,000 equally. Should that allocation of the firm's profits be respected for tax purposes? What factors do you look to evaluate the compensation arrangement?

(b) On her return to Monterey, Eunice married her high school sweetheart and in the second year of her law practice with her father, Eunice had a baby. She took a three-month maternity leave from the law practice. The firm again earned $550,000 of net income and Duffy and Eunice divided that amount as they had the prior year. As a result of Eunice's maternity leave, Duffy billed 60 percent of the total hours billed by the law firm and Eunice billed 40 percent of the total hours. Should the allocation of earnings be respected for tax purposes? What factors do you consider relevant to the determination?

3. (a) Charles Darwin is a professor of biology at Kingston University. As a condition of employment, Charles entered into an agreement with the University that requires him to pay the University 50 percent of any patent royalties derived by Charles as a result of work during his employment at the University. In his laboratory, Charles discovered and patented a genetic marker for the identification of the form of anthrax that affects humans. The patent was licensed to BioTech, Inc., which paid Charles annual royalty fees based on BioTech's sales of a portable device installed in office buildings to detect anthrax. In the current year Charles shared $100,000 of royalty income with Kingston University, with $50,000 going to each. How much of the royalty payments are includable in Charles's gross income?

(b)Does it make a difference if the employment agreement specifies that Kingston University will own the rights to any patent arising from Charles's work while an employee of the University and that the University will pay Charles 50 percent of any royalty income derived from a patent resulting from Charles's work?

SECTION 2. INCOME FROM PROPERTY

1. Lana owns a multistory office building that is leased to several tenants. The whole of the ground floor is leased to the Last National Bank of Cityville. The Last National Bank lease calls for annual rental payments of $60,000 for a ten-year term. The remaining office space in the building produces annual rental income of $120,000.

    (a) Who is taxable on the rental income if Lana assigns the lease to her son Turner for a period of five years? Under the assignment, the Third National Bank pays the rent directly to Turner.

    (b) Who is taxable on the rental income if Lana assigns the Third National Bank lease to Turner for the entire lease term?

    (c) What is the tax consequence to Turner if, after Lana assigns him the lease for the entire lease term, he sells the lease to Donald, who agrees to pay the purchase price in ten equal annual installments of $60,000?

    (d) In lieu of assigning the lease, Lana transfers to Turner an undivided one-third interest in the office building as a gift. Thereafter Turner receives $60,000 of the annual rental income. Who is taxable on the rental income?

2. (a) On April 2, Lana executed a contract to sell her office building to Swanky Realty, Inc. for $1,000,000. The transaction was to close on September 1. Lana's basis in the building is $300,000. On July 1, Lana deeded the building to her son Turner. Between July 1 and September 1, Turner collected the $180,000 rent paid by the building tenants. At the closing on September 1, Swanky Realty paid the $1,000,000 purchase price to Turner. How much income must Lana and Turner each recognize?

    (b) Does your answer change if Lana negotiated the sales contract with Swanky Realty in early March, then deeded the building to Turner, who executed the contract with Swanky Realty on April 2?

SECTION 3. PROPERTY THAT IS THE PRODUCT OF PERSONAL EFFORTS

1. Charles Darwin entered into an agreement with his employer, Kingston University, which provides that any patents produced from Charles's research would belong to the University and that the University would pay Charles 50 percent of any royalty income derived from any such patents. When Charles entered into the employment agreement with Kingston University, Charles also executed a written assignment to his two children, assigning to them any royalty income that should become due to him under his employment agreement. Charles's work produced a patent that generated $50,000 of royalty income in the current year, and pursuant to the agreement $25,000 was paid by Kingston University to Charles's children. Who is taxable on the patent income?

SECTION 4. BELOW-MARKET AND INTEREST-FREE LOANS

1. (a) On January 1, of the current year, Easy Money loaned his son, Funny, $500,000 payable on demand with no interest. Funny used the loan proceeds to purchase a house, which he used as a personal residence. Easy withdrew the money from a money-market fund on which he earned 6 percent interest per year. The applicable federal rate for the year is 5 percent. What are the tax consequences of this loan to Easy and Funny?

(b) What if the amount of the loan were only $90,000, and there were no other loans outstanding between Easy and Funny Money? Funny's only investment income consisted of $100 of interest earned on a checking account.

(c) What if the amount of the loan were only $10,000, and there were no other loans outstanding between Easy and Funny Money, but Funny had investment income of $1,500 for the year?

(d) In part 1(b) Funny Money used the $90,000 loan proceeds to purchase 1000 shares of MicroChip, Inc., which paid a $4,000 dividend in the current year. Funny's only other investment income was $100 of interest earned on a checking account. What is the tax consequence of the loan for Easy and Funny in the current year?

(e) What if the amount of the loan to Funny was $150,000 and Funny used the loan proceeds to purchase 5,000 shares of MicroChip, Inc., which paid a dividend of $20,000 in the current year?

2. Abe owns all of the stock of Broadway Deli Corp. Broadway Deli made a $100,000 interest-free loan to Abe on July 1, Year 8. The loan was unsecured and was for a 10-year term. The applicable federal rate on July 1, 2008 was 7 percent. What are the tax consequences of this loan to Abe and to Broadway Deli Corp.?

CHAPTER 38

TAXATION OF FAMILIES

SECTION 1. THE MARRIED COUPLE AS THE UNIT OF TAXATION

1. (a) Juliet Capulet and Romeo Montague have happily co-habited for several years. They each have $130,000 of taxable income after claiming the standard deduction and a personal exemption. Bowing to parental pressure, Romeo and Juliet decide to get married. What will be the impact of marriage on their combined tax liability? Does your answer depend on the year in which the marriage occurs?

(b) What if Juliet's adjusted gross income was $240,000 and Romeo's adjusted gross income was only $40,400?

(c) After the first year of their marriage, Romeo began associating with some dubious characters and has made some extravagant expenditures, including the purchase of an expensive luxury sports car. Juliet has no idea what the source of this money may be, although she is worried. As her tax advisor, would you advise Juliet to file a joint return with Romeo?

SECTION 2. TAXATION OF CHILDREN AS PART OF THE FAMILY UNIT

1. (a) When Tyger was 10 years old, his grandparents gave him 1,000 shares of stock in DotCom, Inc. The stock has paid annual dividends of $4,000. This year Tyger's parents have taxable income of $500,000. If Tyger is 17 years old this year, at what rate will Tyger's dividend income be taxed?

(b) Tyger also earned $1,000 from babysitting. At what rate will Tyger's babysitting income be taxed?

(c) How would your answer to question 1(a) change if Tyger was 21 years old, was a full time student at Elite University, and was supported by his parents.

SECTION 3. TAX ASPECTS OF DIVORCE AND SEPARATION

1. Juliet became a senior executive in DotCom, Inc. in charge of nanotechnology. In the last few years, Juliet spent much of her time in the Nevada Laboratory of DotCom, leaving Romeo home to take care of the two kids. Romeo filed for a divorce, which Juliet contested.

(a) The divorce decree awarded Romeo $50,000 of spousal support each year for the next five years. Juliet's obligation to pay the support would terminate on Romeo's death. Juliet paid $50,000 the first year, but thereafter failed to make the required payments, paying only $40,000 the next year and $20,000 the year after. How are these payments taxed to Juliet and Romeo?

(b) Would it make a difference if the divorce decree specified that Juliet's payments were in discharge of her interest in their marital property?

(c) What if the divorce decree provided for payments of $50,000 in the first year, $35,000 in the second year, and $25,000 in the third year?

(d) What if the divorce decree specifically provided for support payments of $30,000 per year, which Juliet paid annually, but also provided that the amount of the payments was to be reduced to $20,000 in four years when Romeo and Juliet's oldest child turns age 18, and to $10,000 in five years, when their youngest child turns 18?

(e) The divorce decree also required Juliet to make payments to Healthworks, a health maintenance organization, to provide health coverage for Romeo and each of the two children. Will all or part of these payments be treated as alimony?

(f) In addition, Juliet was required to pay Romeo's attorney fees of $50,000. What is the tax consequence of this payment to Romeo and to Juliet?

(g) As part of the divorce decree, Juliet was required to transfer 10,000 shares of DotCom, Inc. stock to Romeo. Juliet had purchased the stock for $10,000. On the date of the divorce the stock was worth $100,000. Five months after the divorce Romeo sold the stock for $90,000. What are the tax consequences to Romeo and Juliet of the stock transfer? What are the tax consequences to Romeo of the subsequent sale?

(h) What if in exchange for retaining the DotCom stock, Juliet permitted Romeo to keep the family vacation condominium, which was worth $100,000 and which they held as joint tenants. The condominium had cost Romeo and

Juliet $80,000? Five months after the divorce, Romeo sold the condominium for $90,000.

2. Ted and Jane were divorced last year. Pursuant to the divorce decree, Ted transferred 100,000 shares of stock in AOL Corp. to Jane. Ted's basis for the stock was $1,000,000. At the time of transfer, the fair market value of the stock was $6,000,000. Jane sold the stock for $4,000,000. What are the tax consequences to Ted and Jane?

3. Jennifer and Brad were engaged to be married. They entered into an ante-nuptial agreement pursuant to which they both surrendered any rights to alimony or a property settlement upon divorce. Pursuant to the agreement, on December 1, Jennifer transferred to Brad 100,000 shares of stock of Novio Corporation, which had a fair market value of $1,000,000 and for which she had paid $500,000. Two days later, they were married. What are the tax consequences?

SECTION 4. GRANTOR TRUSTS

1. Mr. Horst wants his son, Harrison, who is now 18 years old, to have the use of the interest income from a series of corporate bonds that he owns. He does not want to give up complete ownership of the bonds because he would like Harrison to use the money primarily to help fund his education, so he created the Harrison Trust and transferred the bonds to it. The terms of the trust provide that Mr. Horst will be the Trustee and that all of the income of the trust shall be payable to Harrison.

(a) If the trust instrument provides that after 10 years the trust will terminate and the corpus will be distributed to Mr. Horst, who will be taxed on the income generated by the bonds?

(b) If the trust provides that Mr. Horst may revoke it at any time, who will be taxed on the income generated by the bonds?

(c) If the trust provides that as Trustee, Mr. Horst has the power to withhold distributions of income to Harrison until Harrison is 31 years old or during any period during which Harrison is legally disabled, but he does not otherwise have any ability to alter distributions of income from the trust, who will be taxed on the income generated by the bonds?

(d) If the trust instrument provides that Mr. Horst cannot revoke the trust but Mr. Horst's wife is the Trustee and has the power to terminate the trust at any time, for any reason, and revest ownership of the trust corpus in Mr. Horst, who will be taxed on the income generated by the bonds?

(e) If Harrison is not the beneficiary, the trust is irrevocable, and a bank is the Trustee, but the income is to be used to pay the premiums on insurance on the life of Mr. Horst, who will be taxed on the income generated by the bonds?

2. Assume that Cliff is considering the establishment of a trust the income of which, under § 671 et. seq., will be taxable to him. Can you think of any non-tax reasons why he might want to do that?

PART XI

ALTERNATIVE MINIMUM TAX

CHAPTER 39

ALTERNATIVE MINIMUM TAX FOR INDIVIDUALS

1. (a) Forest, an unmarried bright young attorney in Philadelphia, earned $100,000 as salary during the year. He also incurred expenses of $8,000 in home mortgage interest relating to the acquisition of his house and $5,000 in property taxes paid to Main Line Township with respect to that house. In addition, he paid $4,000 as interest on home equity indebtedness he incurred to buy a car, paid $3,000 in income taxes to the City of Philadelphia, and $2,000 in income taxes to the State of Pennsylvania. As a mark of gratitude to his alma mater, the William Penn University Law School, Forest donated Cherry Computer Corp. stock worth $30,000, which he had bought for $5,000 ten years ago. Assume there is no other relevant information. Which of the foregoing expenses will Forest be able to deduct in computing his taxable income and to what extent? If Forest is subject to the Alternative Minimum

Tax (AMT) what adjustments would have to be made to his taxable income in order to determine his AMTI?

(b) Why do you think Congress has mandated reduction or limitation of some of Forest's deductions in computing AMTI while leaving out the others? Are there any clear-cut distinctions between the items that are to be limited and those that are allowed in full in computing the AMT?

(c) Consider the following additional facts respecting Forest's activities for the year:

(i) Forest spent a week at an American Bar Association Tax Section meeting. His employer did not cover the travel, meals, hotel, and other meeting expenses.

(ii) Forest also earned tax exempt interest from private activity bonds; and

(iii) Forest works in the legal department of a major corporation and had been granted incentive stock options. Forest exercised his options and was able to purchase stock in his employer corporation; the fair market value of the stock far exceeded the amount he paid for it.

Which of these transactions change Forest's AMT liability?

(d) The following year Forest was unfairly fired by his employer. He sued his employer under the § 302 of the Civil Rights Act of 1991 by hiring Gloria Starr, a high profile attorney, and paying her a retainer of $300,000. The case went to trial and a jury awards Forest compensatory damages of $1 million and punitive damages of $4 million. Assume that Forest will be subject to the AMT for that year, that he does not earn any other income during the year, and is entitled to no other deductions. Will Forest be able to deduct the $300,000 retainer paid to Gloria? Would your answer differ if the fee paid to Gloria was $1.5 million and contingent on Forest's receiving an award?

(e)(i) Would your answer differ if instead of suing his employer under the Civil Rights Act, as in Part (d), above, Forest sued his former friend, Billy Bigmouth, for defamation that resulted in Forest's losing his job as an associate in a law firm?

(ii) Would your answer differ if Forest was a self-employed media consultant?

2.Do you agree with the concurring judge in *Klaassen* that the court is powerless to prevent the application of the AMT to taxpayers like the Klaassens? Would your answer differ if the Klaassens had sued for a refund in federal district court and invoked that court's equitable powers?

3.If you served on the staff of the Joint Committee on Taxation and were asked to recommend a solution to the problems wrought by the growth of the AMT, what would you recommend? Why?